THE
HOLY SPIRIT

AN INTRODUCTION

JOHN BEVERE

WITH ADDISON BEVERE

The Holy Spirit: An Introduction
Second Edition
Copyright © 2013, 2014 by John P. Bevere, Jr.

PUBLISHED BY: MESSENGER INTERNATIONAL
P.O. Box 888
Palmer Lake, CO 80133-0888
MessengerInternational.org

Unless otherwise noted, all Scripture quotations are taken from the NEW KING JAMES VERSION®. Copyright © 1982 by Thomas Nelson, Inc. Used by permission. All rights reserved. Scripture quotations marked AMP are taken from the AMPLIFIED® Bible. Copyright © 1954, 1958, 1962, 1964, 1965, 1987 by The Lockman Foundation. Used by permission. (www.Lockman.org) Scripture quotations marked CEV are taken from the CONTEMPORARY ENGLISH VERSION®. Copyright © 1991, 1992, 1995 by American Bible Society. All rights reserved. Scripture quotations marked GNT are taken from the GOOD NEWS TRANSLATION® (Today's English Version, Second Edition). Copyright © 1992 American Bible Society. Used by permission. Scripture quotations marked GW are taken from GOD'S WORD®, © 1995 God's Word to the Nations. Used by permission of Baker Publishing Group. All rights reserved. Scripture quotations marked NASB are taken from the NEW AMERICAN STANDARD BIBLE®, Copyright © 1960, 1962, 1963, 1968, 1971, 1972, 1973, 1975, 1977, 1995 by The Lockman Foundation. Used by permission. (www.Lockman.org) Scripture quotations marked NIV84 are taken from the HOLY BIBLE: NEW INTERNATIONAL VERSION®. Copyright © 1973, 1978, 1984 by International Bible Society. Used by permission of Zondervan Publishing House. All rights reserved. The "NIV" and "New International Version" trademarks are registered in the United States Patent and Trademark Office by International Bible Society. Use of either trademark requires the permission of International Bible Society. Note: Most New International Version Scripture quotations are taken from the 1984 edition and marked NIV84. A few are taken from the 2011 edition: THE HOLY BIBLE, NEW INTERNATIONAL VERSION®, NIV® Copyright © 1973, 1978, 1984, 2011 by Biblica, Inc.™ Used by permission. All rights reserved worldwide. Scripture quotations marked NLT are taken from the Holy Bible, NEW LIVING TRANSLATION. Copyright © 1996, 2004, 2007 by Tyndale House Foundation. Used by permission of Tyndale House Publishers, Inc., Carol Stream, IL 60188. All rights reserved. Note: Some New Living Translation (NLT) Scripture quotations are taken from the first Edition. Scripture quotations marked PHILLIPS are from J.B. Phillips, "The New Testament in Modern English," 1962 edition, published by HarperCollins. Scripture quotations marked The Message are taken from THE MESSAGE. Copyright © 1993, 1994, 1995, 1996, 2000, 2001, 2002. Used by permission of NavPress Publishing Group. Scripture quotations marked TLB are taken from THE LIVING BIBLE. Copyright © 1971 by Tyndale House Publishers, Carol Stream, IL 60188. All rights reserved. Scripture quotations marked (KJV) are taken from the King James Version. Scripture quotations marked NET are from THE NET BIBLE®. Copyright © 2001-2006 by Biblical Studies Press, L.L.C. http://netbible.com. All rights reserved. Used by permission. Scripture quotations marked ESV are from The Holy Bible, ENGLISH STANDARD VERSION® (ESV®), copyright © 2001 by Crossway, a publishing ministry of Good News Publishers. Used by permission. All rights reserved.

Unless otherwise noted, italics and bold treatment used in Scripture and leader quotes indicate the author's added emphasis. Brackets in Scripture versions except those marked (AMP) are the author's parenthetical insertions.

ISBN: 978-1-933185-83-5
ISBN: 978-1-933185-87-3 (electronic)

SPECIAL SALES
Pastors, churches, and ministry leaders can receive special discounts when purchasing Messenger International resources. For information, please visit MessengerInternational.org or call 1-800-648-1477.

DISCUSSION QUESTIONS & DEVOTIONS WRITTEN & EDITED BY:
Vincent M. Newfield, New Fields & Company
P. O. Box 622
Hillsboro, Missouri 63050
www.newfieldscreativeservices.com

COVER, DESIGN & PRINT PRODUCTION:
The Eastco Group
3646 California Rd.
Orchard Park, NY 14127
www.theeastcogroup.com

Front cover artwork: Allan Nygren
Designer: Heather Huether

Printed in Canada

Acknowledgments

To my wife, children, and grandchildren. You are each gifts from God and have brought such richness to my life. I will love you forever and ever.

To my son, Addison, your faith and hard work have enriched this message of the Holy Spirit. It simply would not have been what it is without your help.

To Jaylynn, thank you for your diligence to polish up this message through your excellent editing skills. Your efforts helped to provide both clarity and structure.

To Vincent, thank you for all your hard work in helping us create the devotions. Your work is truly one of a kind.

To the team members and partners of Messenger International, thank you for standing with Lisa and me. We couldn't have asked God for more loyal and true friends to journey with us in reaching out to the nations of the world with the glorious gospel of Jesus Christ.

Most of all, thank You, Father God, for Your unfailing love; and Jesus my King, for giving Your precious life; and You, Holy Spirit, for Your amazing power, comfort, teaching, and intimate fellowship. Thank You for never leaving or forsaking us.

CONTENTS

About This Interactive Book VII

Introduction by Addison Bevere XI

1. Who Is the Holy Spirit? 1

2. The Personality of the Holy Spirit 39

3. Three Levels of Relationships 77

4. Empowered by the Spirit 111

5. The Spirit's Language 155

Bonus Chapter: Q&A with John & Lisa Bevere 199

Appendix: How to Receive Salvation 225

Notes 229

About This Interactive Book

This book may be read cover to cover, just like any other book. However, we encourage you to explore the optional interactive elements for a more personalized experience:

Each chapter of this book is divided into five suggested daily readings with corresponding devotions at the end of the chapter. You can choose to complete one reading and one devotion per day, or you can adapt these elements to your preference. We suggest that those participating in a group study complete the reading and devotions for one chapter per week.

If you are reading this book as part of the Messenger Series study on *The Holy Spirit: An Introduction*, we recommend that you watch or listen to each week's teaching session and answer the discussion questions as a group. Then, read the chapter in the book and complete the devotions. There is one teaching session for each chapter in this book. Discussion questions for each chapter are located after the daily devotions.

Enjoy!

MESSENGER SERIES

MSeries.tv

This book is part of the Messenger Series study on *The Holy Spirit: An Introduction.*

Receive $10 off the purchase of the full curriculum or audio/video sessions*. Visit MSeries.tv and use 'TH54DL' at checkout.

*Applies to physical and digital resources.

Introduction

When my dad first asked me to help him with this book, I was immediately struck by a sense of disbelief. I thought, *He probably hasn't prayed about this yet*. Frankly I did not see myself as a worthy candidate. In fact, thinking about his request caused my stomach to flare like it was in the middle of a breakdancing competition.

I respectfully asked my dad to consider a few alternatives and to spend some serious time praying over the matter (maybe a year or two). Yet after a day of prayer, he was confident that I was the one for the task. It is important to him that the Holy Spirit does not become taboo amongst the younger generations, and he values my input as someone in his mid-twenties. My father and I know that many people—both young and old—will avoid this topic if they don't understand who the Spirit is and how He functions.

So, despite my apprehensions, how could I refuse my father's request? I was compelled to agree. What then transpired can only be described as a life-transforming journey. I began to see the Scriptures in a new light as God opened my eyes to many wonders of His Spirit. I soon discovered that the Holy Spirit is the most misunderstood Person in the Church. Countless labels and stereotypes have been assigned to Him, but too few of us know Him as He really is.

The purpose of this book is to facilitate an introduction to the Person of the Holy Spirit by taking you on a journey through the Scriptures. Aspects of this book may be challenging, but I promise you that the journey is worth your time and energy.

As you read the words on these pages, ask the Holy Spirit to guide you into all truth. He will remove any beliefs that are not grounded in His Word. You will discover that He does not "belong" to a denomination or a movement—and that He cannot be confined to a generation or an age. He has been sent to reveal Jesus and empower the entire Body of Christ. He has made our hearts His home, and He has promised to make good out of our lives. All we have to do is give Him control.

A better friend and companion cannot be found. The Holy Spirit will faithfully accompany you through all of life's struggles and joys. He has promised to never leave or forsake you because you are His passion and delight. Get ready to discover the One who is the definition of awesome!

—Addison Bevere, COO, Messenger International

Now all of us can come to the Father through the same
Holy Spirit because of what Christ has done for us.
(Ephesians 2:18 NLT)

1

Who Is the Holy Spirit?

*But the Comforter (Counselor, Helper, Intercessor, Advocate, Strengthener, Standby), **the Holy Spirit**, Whom the Father will send in My name [in My place, to represent Me and act on My behalf], He will teach you all things. And He will cause you to recall (will remind you of, bring to your remembrance) everything I have told you.*

—John 14:26 AMP

Day 1

It was the eve of a new year. An urge to fast and pray stirred within. I asked the Lord, "What book of the Bible should I read?" To my surprise I heard, "The book of Acts."

Why was I surprised? Because my previous time of extended fasting and prayer had also been met with this exact directive: "Read the book of Acts." During my previous fast, what stood out in Acts was a conflict of purpose and direction in the life of the apostle Paul, and its resulting consequences of hardship. Allow me to explain.

Paul was chosen by God to preach the gospel to the Gentiles. He said, "I was appointed a preacher, an apostle, and a teacher of the Gentiles" (2 Timothy 1:11). This is a specific and focused directive. He repeated this mandate several times throughout the course of his life. Early in his first apostolic journey he stated to the Jews, "We turn to the Gentiles. For so the Lord has commanded us: 'I have set you as a light to the Gentiles'" (Acts 13:46-47). During his second journey, he boldly stated, "From now on I will go to the Gentiles" (Acts 18:6). To the Romans he wrote, "I am an apostle to the Gentiles" (11:13). These statements continue throughout his writings.

However, out of his love and desire to see his Jewish countrymen saved, he repeatedly sought out the synagogues in almost every city he visited. He habitually approached the Jews before attempting to reach the Gentiles; in fact, it was often the Jewish rejection of his message that drove him to the Gentiles. As it turned out, the Jews were the source of Paul's greatest persecution and trouble. They stirred up the populace and created animosity between the apostle and the Gentile leaders. Their divisive schemes were behind most of the riots, arrests, beatings, and trials Paul faced. An important note: God cares deeply for the Jews. This is why James, Peter, and John were sent to them: "James, Peter, and John, who were known as pillars of the church...encouraged us to keep preaching to the Gentiles, while they continued their work with the Jews" (Galatians 2:9 NLT).

The message revealed to me during my previous fast was abundantly clear: "Son, stay within the sphere of grace that I've called you to walk in. Don't allow your natural affections or love to pull you away from the divine assignment on your life." Remembering this encounter with such clarity, it was surprising that God asked me to read through Acts again. After all, there were sixty-five other books to choose from!

I'm so glad I obeyed, for this time as I journeyed through Acts, something completely different stood out to me (demonstrating that the Word of God is truly alive). This time, what jumped off the pages was how much the leaders and members of the early Church looked to, interacted with, depended on, and spoke of the Holy Spirit. He was a vital part of their lives and involved in everything they did. He was preeminent in their ministry outreaches, team gatherings, and strategy meetings, and He was always involved in their activities. Here's a sampling of the statements that stood out:

- "Why has Satan filled your heart to lie to the Holy Spirit?" (Acts 5:3)
- "How is it that you have agreed together to test the Spirit of the Lord?" (Acts 5:9)
- "We are His witnesses to these things, and so also is the Holy Spirit." (Acts 5:32)
- "You always resist the Holy Spirit." (Acts 7:51)
- "The Spirit told me to go with them." (Acts 11:12)
- "One of them…showed by the Spirit that there was going to be a great famine…" (Acts 11:28)
- "Being sent out by the Holy Spirit…" (Acts 13:4)
- "For it seemed good to the Holy Spirit, and to us…" (Acts 15:28)
- "They were forbidden by the Holy Spirit to preach the word in Asia." (Acts 16:6)
- "They tried to go into Bithynia, but the Spirit did not permit them." (Acts 16:7)
- "Paul was compelled by the Spirit, and testified…" (Acts 18:5)
- "Did you receive the Holy Spirit when you believed?" (Acts 19:2)
- "Paul felt compelled by the Spirit to go over to Macedonia." (Acts 19:21 NLT)
- "The Holy Spirit tells me in city after city…" (Acts 20:23 NLT)
- "Take heed to yourselves and to all the flock, among which the Holy Spirit has made you overseers." (Acts 20:28)

Words like these jumped off the pages repeatedly. What became painfully clear is the reality that we are not seeing this same pattern in the Church today. What was common among the believers in Acts seems rare now. I am not just addressing this lack in the lives of others, but first and foremost the lack in my own life. As I read, I realized I had drawn back from enjoying, seeking out, and depending on the leadership, camaraderie, interaction, and powerful influence of the Spirit of God. Once this became clear to me, how could I keep from sharing it with you?

Upfront Statements

Allow me to make some upfront statements that will become clearer the more we delve into this important discussion:

First, there is virtually no Christian life without the Holy Spirit.
- Without the Holy Spirit, Christianity is dry, monotonous, and mundane.
- Without the Holy Spirit, our labor is draining and wearisome.
- Without the Holy Spirit, there is no fellowship with God.

Remove the Holy Spirit from a church and one of two things will happen:
- It will morph into a social club.
- It will become a religious institution.

The truth is...
- There is no revelation without the Holy Spirit. In fact, without the Spirit Scripture becomes lethal; for we are told, "the letter kills, but the Spirit gives life" (2 Corinthians 3:6).
- There is no vision without the Holy Spirit.
- There is no joy without Him.
- There is no peace without Him.
- There is no freedom without the Holy Spirit.

The Lord is the Spirit, and wherever the Spirit of the Lord is, there is freedom. (2 Corinthians 3:17 NLT)

Look at the words "wherever the Spirit of the Lord is." Let's think this through. God's Spirit is omnipresent—He's everywhere at all times. David states, "Where can I go from Your Spirit? Or where can I flee from Your presence?" (Psalm 139:7). The answer is emphatically, *nowhere*. David continues to write, "If I climb to the sky, you're there! If I go underground, you're there! If I flew on morning's wings to the far western horizon, you'd find me in a minute—you're already there waiting!" (Psalm 139:8-10 The Message). It's crystal clear, He is *everywhere* at all times.

So the next question we must ask is, "Is there freedom *everywhere?*" Look again at Paul's words: "Wherever the Spirit of the Lord is, there is freedom." We have proven that He is *everywhere*; so again, is there freedom *everywhere?* The answer to this is, absolutely no. There isn't freedom in brothels, bars, prisons, and hospitals. I've been to neighborhoods, schools, homes, and even churches where there is no freedom. So what is Scripture declaring here? I suggest that this would be a more accurate translation:

Wherever the Spirit is *Lord*, that's where there is freedom.
(2 Corinthians 3:17, author's paraphrase)

The Greek word *lord* is *kyrios*. It is defined as "supreme in authority."[1] The Holy Spirit is not permitted to be in authority in most bars, prisons, hospitals, or homes, and even in many churches. Where He is welcomed as supreme in authority, that is where you will find freedom and justice for all.

The Purpose of This Message

The purpose of this message is to introduce you to the *Person* of the Holy Spirit. Volumes and volumes could be written about Him. Days, months, even years could be spent speaking of Him.

I have been married to my wife, Lisa, for over thirty years. As well as I know her, I am still discovering aspects of her personality, interests, desires, and mannerisms I have never known. Recently we spent a few days alone together celebrating our thirtieth wedding anniversary. During that time, I learned aspects of her dreams, preferences, and even abilities that I never knew existed.

In regard to abilities, I had no idea how naturally talented Lisa is in golf. She knows how much I enjoy the sport, so she offered to accompany me on the back nine of a beautiful golf course. (I only played one round because it was our time together.) There was a huge chasm on the seventeenth hole. My wife always loves a good challenge, so I asked her if she wanted to attempt to get the ball over. It would take a 150-yard shot to clear the 200-foot deep chasm; if the shot fell short, the ball would be lost in the ocean. I found an old ball for Lisa to use (because I didn't think I would ever see it again). She stood up on the tee box and cracked it 175 yards into the fairway on the other side. Alas, after thirty years of marriage, a new talent had been discovered.

During our dinner each night, Lisa shared knowledge, wisdom, interests, and longings that she had not shared with me before. In short, I was in awe of how much depth there is to this amazing woman whom I get to call my wife.

It would be impossible to share the full knowledge of Lisa in a few short chapters. It couldn't be done in volumes. However, what I can do is tell you how to contact and converse with her. I can share what she enjoys, her interests, and how to work and interact with her. I can tell you her strengths, weaknesses, and what she loves or doesn't care for. This introductory knowledge would serve as a catalyst to a great relationship with her.

If it's impossible to completely tell you about Lisa, who's only decades old, then how could I come close to fully telling you about the Holy Spirit, when He is from everlasting to everlasting? I simply could not! But what I can do is introduce you to who He is. I can tell you about His personality, what interests Him, and what He loves. I can define our relationship with Him and share some ways that we can engage and interact with Him. I can tell you why our relationship with the Holy Spirit is so important and how He empowers us to fulfill God's desires for our lives. These basic insights could propel you into a deeper, more meaningful relationship with Him.

Day 2

A Serious Misconception

There is an error that many make: they have attempted to understand the *work* and *power* of the Holy Spirit without first coming to know Him as a *Person*.

It is crucial that we establish in our hearts and minds whether we believe that the Holy Spirit is a divine Person—One who is infinitely holy, infinitely wise, and infinitely mighty, yet wonderfully tender, sensitive, and compassionate. Do we believe He is One who is worthy to receive our reverence, affection, faith, love, devotion, and complete surrender? Or do we instead believe that the Holy Spirit is simply an influence proceeding from God—some sort of divine mystical power, not unlike what we think of when we refer to "the spirit of generosity" or "the spirit of competition"?

This latter view is shallow, crude, and even cultic. If we believe this way, we are easily susceptible to spiritual haughtiness or pride, which would lead us to strut about as if we belong to some higher order of Christianity.

However, if we see Him as infinite in majesty, glory, splendor, wisdom, knowledge, and holiness, and if we believe that He, as a Person, has an accord with the Father and Son to take possession of our lives and make good out of them, then we will fall on our faces in holy awe.

Someone who sees God's Spirit as an influence or supreme power will constantly say, "I want more of the Spirit." On the contrary, someone who sees Him as a wonderful Person will say, "How can I give more of myself to Him?"[2]

Our Perception of Him

One of the reasons many perceive the Spirit of God as a mere influence, rather than as a Person, is the way He's been spoken of. Have you ever heard anyone refer to the Holy Spirit as an "it"? I have been in ministry for thirty years; if I were given a dollar for each time I've heard the Spirit of God referred to as an "it," I would be very wealthy. Unfortunately, so many of us miss out on the fullness of the Spirit's presence because we refuse to honor Him as a Person. The Spirit of God will not manifest where He's not honored (see Matthew 13:54-58; Psalm 89:7).

I want to note that in calling the Holy Spirit a "Person," I am not calling Him human. What I am simply saying is that He possesses attributes of what we would consider to be personality. The Holy Spirit is Deity, not a human being. But we must remember, humans were created in God's image. So He's not like us; rather, we are like Him.

As a Church, we've chosen to view Him as a "holy entity" rather than as One who is *most holy*. His desire is to be our closest friend, yet we have limited His involvement in our lives. The sad truth is we have inadvertently rejected the most fulfilling relationship available to us.

Let's take a look at some scriptures that will perfectly illustrate the personality of the Holy Spirit:

- He has a mind (see Romans 8:27).
- He has a will (see 1 Corinthians 12:11).
- He has emotions, such as love and joy (see Romans 15:30; Galatians 5:22).
- He comforts (see Acts 9:31).
- He speaks (see Hebrews 3:7); in fact, He speaks clearly (see 1 Timothy 4:1).
- He teaches (see 1 Corinthians 2:13).
- He can be made to feel sorrow (see Ephesians 4:30).
- He can be insulted (see Hebrews 10:29).
- He can be resisted (see Acts 7:51).
- He can be lied to (see Acts 5:1-11).

If these attributes are so apparent in Scripture, then we must ask, why is the Holy Spirit so misunderstood?

The Dove

When many people think of the Holy Spirit, their minds immediately draw an association with a dove. Why is this often the first association? Did the Holy Spirit ever manifest as a dove? The answer is an emphatic *no*. In all four Gospels we read that the Spirit of God descended on Jesus *like a dove* (see Matthew 3:16; Mark 1:10; Luke 3:22; John 1:32).

But don't we often make comments like "she runs like the wind" or "he is strong like an ox"? If I say that my son is strong like an ox, does that make him a four-footed animal? Absolutely not! Similarly, to say that the Spirit descended like a dove is not to say that He is a dove.

Someone might say, "Yes, but John, He's represented as flames before the throne of God" (see Revelation 4:5). Yes, this is the case, but the Bible also says, "I looked, and behold...in the midst of the elders, stood a lamb as though it had been slain..." (Revelation 5:6). This is John's description of Jesus. You and I both know that Jesus is certainly not a four-footed animal. In the same way, the Holy Spirit is not a mystical fire burning in front of God's throne.

So, Who Is the Holy Spirit?

The Bible makes it very clear that the Holy Spirit is the third Person of the Godhead. Genesis 1:26 says, "Then God said, 'Let *Us* make man in *Our* image, according to *Our* likeness.'" Notice that God did not say, "Let Me make man." The drama of creation required three distinct Actors playing three distinct parts; God was referring to Himself as the Father, the Son, and the Holy Spirit.

Let's look at Acts 10:38 to see the distinct identification of the Father, the Son, and the Holy Spirit.

> *God* anointed *Jesus* of Nazareth with the *Holy Spirit* and with power, who went about doing good and healing all who were oppressed by the devil, for God was with Him.

In this verse, we witness the *Father* anointing *Jesus* with the *Holy Spirit*—three distinct Persons working together for one common purpose.

Let's look at another example:

> When He had been baptized, *Jesus* came up immediately from
> the water; and behold, the heavens were opened to Him, and
> He saw the *Spirit of God* descending like a dove and alighting
> upon Him. And suddenly *a voice* came from heaven, saying,
> "This is My beloved Son, in whom I am well pleased."
> (Matthew 3:16-17)

In this account of Jesus' baptism, you will notice once again the
members of the Godhead manifest as three distinct Persons. First, *Jesus*
was baptized by John, then the *Spirit of God* descended on Him, and
finally *God the Father* declared from heaven, "This is My beloved Son
in whom I'm well pleased." Again, all three members working together
for the same purpose.

Let me offer a basic example that will help illustrate this truth.
Water (H_2O) can manifest as three different forms. Temperature de-
termines whether H_2O will appear as a solid, liquid, or gas. Water's
substance—its molecular structure—never changes one iota, but its
expression will change based on its environment (the temperature). In
the same way, God's central makeup doesn't change. When you see the
Son, you see the Father; and the Spirit was sent to reveal the Son to us
(see John 17:21; Ephesians 1:17-18). God is one in purpose, and yet He
has three expressions (Persons) who perform unique functions. Though
there are three Persons, there is only one God. Deuteronomy 6:4 says,
"Hear, O Israel: the Lord our God, the Lord is one!" Romans 3:30
says, "There is one God who will justify." James 2:19 likewise says, "You
believe that there is one God. You do well." This truth is a cornerstone
for the rest of the book: there are three distinct divine Persons, but only
one God.

Day 3

The First Person

The Holy Spirit is actually the first member of the Godhead who appears in the Bible. Genesis chapter one reads, "In the beginning God created the heavens and the earth" (verse 1). Now, let's look at verse two: "The earth was without form, and void; and darkness was on the face of the deep. And the Spirit of God was hovering over the face of the waters." The Spirit shows up right here in Genesis 1:2; He is the first member of the Godhead to be mentioned by name.

The question could be asked, "But John, in verse one it says, 'In the beginning God created the heavens and the earth.' How can you say the Holy Spirit is the first member of the Godhead mentioned in Scripture if the first verse mentions God the Father?" That's an excellent question. But remember, God said, "Let Us create man in Our image." The reference to God in verse one refers to the Godhead, not to a specific member of the Godhead. Therefore, the first member of the Godhead identified by function is actually the Holy Spirit. In verse two we read that "the Spirit of God [the Holy Spirit] was hovering over the face of the waters."

Again, let's go back to our original question: who is the Holy Spirit? I can attest that He is the most amazing, wonderful, kind, tender, sensitive, mighty Person on the face of the earth. You may reply, "John, on the face of the earth?" Oh yes, on the face of the earth. What we have to understand is that the Father is not here on the earth; He's on His throne in heaven. Likewise, Jesus is not here on the earth. I hear people say all the time, "Jesus is in my heart," yet Scripture makes it very clear that He is seated at the right hand of God (see Mark 16:19). In Acts 1:9-11 we read:

While [the disciples] watched, He was taken up, and a cloud received Him out of their sight. And while they looked...toward heaven...two men stood by them in white apparel, who also said, "Men of Galilee, why do you stand gazing up into heaven? This same Jesus, who was taken up from you into heaven, will so come in like manner as you saw Him go into heaven."

The two men, who were actually angels, made it clear to the disciples that Jesus would return in the same way He left. In other words, He's not going to return to earth until He comes in the clouds. Has Jesus returned in the clouds yet? The answer is clearly no. This means presently Jesus is still at the right hand of God in heaven.

Think about the time when Stephen was stoned. We read in Acts 7:55-56, "But [Stephen], being full of the Holy Spirit, gazed into heaven and saw the glory of God, and Jesus standing at the right hand of God, and said, 'Look! I see the heavens opened and the Son of Man standing at the right hand of God!'" Try to imagine Jesus in all His glory standing in honor of His martyr, anticipating this sacred moment that would be recounted for generations to come. While this story is a beautiful depiction of a glorious reunion, it also serves as a reminder of the irrefutable fact that Jesus currently resides at His Father's side.

The truth is that Jesus has been in this position of glory for approximately two thousand years. He's not here on the earth. I know we like to say He lives in our hearts, but in reality, the Holy Spirit, the Spirit of Jesus Christ, is the One who makes our hearts His dwelling place.

It is important for us to recognize that the Holy Spirit is referred to as both the Spirit of God the Father and the Spirit of Jesus Christ (the Son). Let's take a look at some examples of this.

In Philippians 1:19 Paul states, "For I know that this will turn out for my deliverance through your prayer and the supply of *the Spirit of Jesus Christ.*" Jesus made it abundantly clear that He would have to leave so that the Holy Spirit could come in His place. Paul is clearly referring to the Holy Spirit (the Helper) here, not to the incarnate Jesus, because Jesus is no longer on the earth.

In Matthew 10:20 Jesus declares, "For it is not you who speak, but *the Spirit of your Father* who speaks in you." Jesus was speaking of the time to come when His disciples would be persecuted and tried for the gospel's sake. The Spirit of the Father (the Holy Spirit) would guide them and put the right words in their mouths.

Even now, as I write, these words are not the result of my intellect or experience. The Spirit of my Father is teaching through me. I have tried to teach out of my own strength; trust me, it only ends in miserable failure. It is by His grace, the empowerment of His Holy Spirit, that I am what I am. The good news is He has never left me high and dry— He always shows up. When I yield in humility to the Spirit of grace (see Hebrews 10:29), He is faithful to turn my weakness into strength.

How Do the Three Work?

This "three in one" concept can be very difficult to grasp because it defies our human understanding. First Corinthians 12:5-7 offers some insight into how the Three work together as One.

> And there are differences of administrations, but the same Lord. And there are diversities of operations, but it is the same God which worketh all in all. But the manifestation of the Spirit is given to every man to profit withal. (1 Corinthians 12:5-7 KJV)

As we read this passage, we discover that the Father, the Son, and the Holy Spirit all serve different roles. The Father operates or initiates (verse 6), the Son administrates (verse 5), and the Holy Spirit manifests (verse 7); yet all of them work together for the same purpose.

If you and I were going to build a house, what would we need to do? Well, we would need to hire an architect, a foreman, and workers (subcontractors) to actually build the house. In this illustration, God the Father is the architect, Jesus is the foreman, and the Holy Spirit is represented by the workers who build the house—He's the *"manifester"* of creation. All three roles are essential to the construction of any house.

The Finger of God

Let's take a look at two different scriptural accounts of the same incident. Jesus has just healed a demon-possessed man. The people are astonished, but the Pharisees think to themselves, *He is only casting out demons by the devil himself* (see Matthew 12:23-24). In verse 28 we read Jesus' response to their thoughts: "If I cast out devils by the Spirit of God, then the kingdom of God is come unto you" (KJV).

Luke also provides a record of this declaration, but his account differs slightly from Matthew's. Luke 11:20 states, "But if I *with the finger of God* cast out devils, no doubt the kingdom of God is come upon you" (KJV). Both Luke and Matthew are referring to the Holy Spirit. As writers often do, Luke is describing the Holy Spirit's function as opposed to His Person. Therefore we can deduce that the Holy Spirit can be described as the "finger of God."

Not only is the Holy Spirit's function identified as the finger of God, but also the *hand of God*, and the *arm of God*. Scripture states that God delivered His people "with a strong hand and an outstretched arm" (Psalm 136:12 NASB). Psalm 8:3 declares, "When I consider Your heavens, *the work of Your fingers*, the moon and the stars, which You have ordained..." Most believers don't realize that the Holy Spirit is the One who actually put the stars and the planets in the heavens; He's the One who manifested all of creation. Remember, in Genesis 1:2 we read, "...the Spirit of God was hovering over the face of the waters." He was waiting for the Father to initiate. The Son then had to administrate by saying, "Light be," because Jesus is the Word of God. When "light be" was spoken, the Son administered the Father's will and the Holy Spirit created that which was spoken.

One of my favorite passages on the magnitude and glory of the Spirit of God is Isaiah 40:12-15. It reads:

Who else has held the oceans in his hand? Who has measured off the heavens with his fingers? Who else knows the weight of the earth or has weighed the mountains and hills on a scale? Who is able to advise the Spirit of the Lord? Who knows enough to give him advice or teach him? Has the Lord ever needed anyone's advice? Does he need instruction about what is good? Did someone teach him what is right or show him the path of justice? No, for all the nations of the world are but a drop in the bucket. They are nothing more than dust on the scales. He picks up the whole earth as though it were a grain of sand. (Isaiah 40:12-15 NLT)

In verse twelve we read, "Who has measured off the heavens with His fingers?" So you can see the Holy Spirit is being identified by His function. And think about it. The Spirit of the Lord held the entire ocean. Do you see how mighty He is? And yet He has humbled Himself by agreeing with the Father and the Son to come and make His residence in us. What an amazing, awe-inspiring reality!

The Holy Spirit Is God

Let's take a look at the role the Holy Spirit played during the creation of man. We read, "And the Lord God formed man of the dust of the ground, and breathed into his nostrils the breath of life; and man became a living being" (Genesis 2:7). The Holy Spirit is the One who actually formed Adam and breathed life into his nostrils. How do I know this to be true? Job 33:4 states, "The Spirit of God has made me, and the breath of the Almighty gives me life." The Holy Spirit not only formed and breathed life into Adam's nostrils, He also formed and breathed life into you and me. Psalm 139:13 says, "You formed my inward parts; You covered me in my mother's womb." In fact, the Spirit of God formed everything we see, for Proverbs 26:10 says, "The great God who formed everything…" The creation we see was manifested because the Holy Spirit enacted the creative desire of the Father.

I hope it is evident to you that the Holy Spirit is God. Let's take a look at some of the different names used for Him in scripture. He's called:

- Holy Spirit (96 times)
- Spirit of the Lord (28 times)
- Spirit of God (26 times)
- Eternal Spirit (Hebrews 9:14)
- Helper (4 times by Jesus in John's Gospel)

- Comforter (used throughout the *Amplified Bible*)
- Holy One (Psalm 78:41)
- The Lord (2 Corinthians 3:17)
- Spirit of truth (4 times)
- Spirit of Christ (Romans 8:9; 1 Peter 1:11)
- Spirit of Jesus Christ (Philippians 1:19)
- Spirit of counsel (Isaiah 11:2)
- Spirit of knowledge (Isaiah 11:2)
- Spirit of might (Isaiah 11:2)
- Spirit of understanding (Isaiah 11:2)
- Spirit of wisdom (Isaiah 11:2)
- Spirit of the fear of the Lord (Isaiah 11:2)
- Spirit of your Father (Matthew 10:20)
- Spirit of glory (1 Peter 4:14)
- Spirit of grace (Zechariah 12:10; Hebrews 10:29)
- Spirit of judgment (Isaiah 4:4)
- Spirit of burning (Isaiah 4:4)
- Spirit of life (Romans 8:2)
- Spirit of love (2 Timothy 1:7)
- Spirit of power (2 Timothy 1:7)
- Spirit of a sound mind (2 Timothy 1:7)
- Spirit of prophecy (Revelation 19:10)
- Spirit of revelation (Ephesians 1:17)
- Spirit of holiness (Romans 1:4)
- Spirit of the Holy God (4 times in Daniel)

He is worthy, He is mighty, and He is awesome!

Jesus Totally Depended on the Holy Spirit

Jesus was completely dependent on the Holy Spirit. He was conceived by the Spirit, He was taught by the Spirit, He was empowered by the Spirit at the Jordan river, and He didn't do one miracle until He was baptized with the Spirit (see John's account of the first miracle Jesus did in Canaan of Galilee: John 1:29-34 and 2:1-11). He was led by the Spirit, and He only spoke what He heard the Spirit speaking.

In John 14:10 Jesus says, "The words that I speak to you I do not speak on My own authority; but *the Father who dwells in Me* does the works." Notice Jesus did not say "the Father in heaven." He said "the Father who dwells in Me."

Wait a minute, John, do you mean Jesus is referring to the Holy Spirit as His Father? Well, why wouldn't He? Listen to what the angel said to Joseph: "Do not be afraid to take Mary as your wife. For the child within her was conceived by the Holy Spirit" (Matthew 1:20 NLT). Jesus was conceived by the Holy Spirit, so it makes sense that He would refer to the Holy Spirit as "the Father who dwells in Me."

The truth is, Jesus and the Holy Spirit always worked together during Jesus' time on earth. In fact, Jesus made this statement: "The Son can do nothing by Himself" (John 5:19 NLT). If Jesus—the Son of God Himself—needed this ongoing partnership with the Holy Spirit to complete His mission, how much more do we need the Spirit to help us complete our missions?

No one knows the Holy Spirit better than Jesus, so let's take a look at what Jesus said about the Holy Spirit's role, personality, attributes, power, and other abilities in our lives. In John 14:15-18, Jesus declares:

If you love Me, keep My commandments. And I will pray the
Father, and He will give you another Helper, that He may

abide with you forever—the Spirit of truth, whom the world
cannot receive, because it neither sees Him nor knows Him;
but you know Him, for He dwells with you and will be in you.
I will not leave you orphans; I will come to you.

There are so many nuggets in this passage. First, you'll notice Jesus said, "If you love Me, keep My commandments." It's interesting that Jesus prefaces His comments about the Holy Spirit with a reminder to recognize Jesus' supreme authority, His lordship. He places a huge emphasis on our obedience in keeping His commandments. Peter confirms this truth: "We are His witnesses to these things, and so also is the Holy Spirit *whom God has given to those who obey Him*" (Acts 5:32). God gives the Holy Spirit to those who obey Him.

Now notice that Jesus says in John 14:16, "I will pray the Father, and He will give you *another* Helper." Let's take a look at the Greek word for *another*. There are two Greek words that are translated into our English word *another* throughout the New Testament. These Greek words are *heteros* and *allos*. *Heteros* means "another of a *different* sort." *Allos* means "another of the *same* kind."[3] The question we have to ask is, which word is Jesus using here?

Before I give you the answer, let me provide an example that will illustrate the difference between these two Greek words. Imagine this scenario: I hand you a piece of fruit, an apple for instance. After you have eaten the apple, I ask you, "Would you like another piece of fruit?"

Now if you reply, "Yes," and I proceed to give you an orange, I gave you "another." However, I gave you *another of a different sort*. An orange is a type of fruit, but it is a different sort of fruit than an apple. This is an example of *heteros*.

Now if you asked for another piece of fruit and I gave you a second apple, then you would say I gave you *another of the same kind*. This is an example of *allos*.

So let's return to the original question. When Jesus says the Father will give us "another" Helper, which word is He using? He is using the word *allos*. So He is saying, "The Father is going to give you another Helper who is just like Me." In other words, Jesus is saying that He and the Holy Spirit are of the same kind.

Our Lifelong Companion

Another word Jesus uses in John 14:16 is the word *Helper*. The Greek word for *helper* here is *parakletos*. Jesus is also referred to as *parakletos* in an Epistle of John: "My little children…we have an Advocate [*parakletos*] with the Father, Jesus Christ the righteous" (1 John 2:1). Both Jesus and the Holy Spirit perform this role of helper or *parakletos*. So what does this Greek word mean? In the vernacular of the day, it was used to describe a lawyer who pled someone's case.[4] It was also used to describe a personal counselor or a coach—a life coach.

Parakletos is a compound word of two Greek words, *para* and *kaleo*. *Para* means "very close."[5] Paul used this word to describe his relationship with Timothy. There was nobody closer to Paul than the apostle Timothy (see Philippians 2:20). My wife, Lisa, is *para* to me. There is nobody on the face of the earth who is closer to me than she is. I would use that word in describing my relationship with her.

The second Greek word, *kaleo*, means "to beckon or to call."[6] This word was frequently used in Scripture when the apostles were describing their callings. For example, when Paul said, "I am *called* an apostle to the Gentiles," he was using the Greek word *kaleo*. The concept of a "call" invokes thoughts of destiny and action.

When we put these two Greek words together, we get a much better understanding of what Jesus is communicating. Essentially, He is saying that *the Holy Spirit is permanently called closely alongside each of us to provide coaching, direction, instruction, and counsel in our life journey.* This is His calling, or assignment, and He perpetually journeys with us to help, never tiring! Jesus said that the Holy Spirit would abide with us forever (John 14:16). He will never leave nor forsake us. What an amazing promise! Jesus is essentially saying that the Holy Spirit will be a continuation of His (Jesus') exact work and mission in our lives.

Frequently I hear people say, "Oh, if only I could have walked with Jesus, I would have asked Him so many questions." Why not present those questions to the Holy Spirit? This is a crucial area where our perceptions of the Holy Spirit come into play. If we simply perceive Him as an ambiguous entity, we will not approach Him as One who is capable of teaching or coaching us. The Holy Spirit is Deity, not an entity. If we truly believe He is who the Word of God says He is, we will approach Him in reverence knowing that He is the all-knowing and all-powerful One who is willing and able to teach, help, and coach us. Yes, He longs to speak intimately with us.

Sadly, the Holy Spirit is probably the most ignored Person in the Church. How many times are we gathered together and He is not honored or even mentioned? How often do we go through our morning, afternoon, evening, or even entire day and not say one word to the One who is permanently called to reside in us and walk with us?

A Startling Statement

Jesus made a mind-blowing statement in John 16:7: "Nevertheless I tell you the truth..."

Before we continue with this passage, let me take a moment to paint a picture for you. This is Jesus speaking to His disciples. He has been with these guys for over three years. Everything He has ever said has come to pass. He said, "Wind be still," and it was still. He said, "You're going to find a donkey in a certain place" and sure enough, the donkey was there. He knew there was a traitor on his staff before the traitor ever manifested. He told a fig tree to die, and it shriveled up within twenty-four hours. Everything that Jesus said had come to pass, and yet He had to preface this statement with, "Nevertheless I tell you the truth." Basically, what Jesus was about to say was going to blow His disciples' minds, so He had to make sure they knew He was telling them the truth.

So what does Jesus go on to say? "Nevertheless I tell you the truth. It is to your advantage that I go away; for if I do not go away, the Helper [*parakletos*] will not come to you; but if I depart, I will send Him to you" (John 16:7). The New Living Translation reads, "It is best for you that I go away."

Put yourself in the disciples' shoes. Your leader, who you know to be the Son of God, has just told you that He needs to leave you—and that His departure is for your benefit. That would sound crazy to me. If He is God, wouldn't it be most to your benefit for Him to stay? I'm sure the disciples were thinking the same thing. For this exact reason, Jesus prefaced this statement with, "I tell you the truth."

So why was it best for the disciples and the generations of believers to come—including you and me—that Jesus went away? Consider this. If Jesus never left the earth, then the Holy Spirit would never have come alongside us. If I wanted to receive something from Jesus, I would have to travel many miles just to see Him. My journey would probably begin with a flight to Tel Aviv (which would be the busiest airport in the world). I would then need to rent a car, drive to Galilee, and hope to find some kind of decent accommodation (the hotels would be completely full). Then I'd have to find Jesus. It wouldn't be hard because millions of people would be waiting to speak with Him. After finding

Him, I'd have to wade through the most complex system of lines ever known to mankind, because everyone would want to ask Jesus a question or present Him with a request.

Since there would be such a long line, I would probably be limited to a maximum of sixty seconds with Jesus, so I would definitely need to have my questions or requests ready. And remember, He would need to sleep and eat, so He would have maybe a good fourteen hours per day to give to the masses. At this rate, Jesus would be able to see 840 people a day if he spent 60 seconds with each person. It would therefore take Jesus 1,190 days (3.26 years) to see a million people. But keep in mind that new people would constantly be joining the stream—and what if there were a "fast pass" line for those with really urgent needs and requests? These people would always be going in front of me, right? I think we can surmise that getting to Jesus would be nearly impossible and definitely improbable.

The good news is the Holy Spirit is *always* there for us. He doesn't have to sleep or eat. He can carry on billions of conversations at the same time with billions of different people. When we allow our understanding of the Holy Spirit to be radically transformed by the Word of God, we will begin to understand why Jesus could say, "It is better for you that I go away."

Remember, the Holy Spirit is just like Jesus: He teaches like Jesus, He amplifies the things of God like Jesus, and He is here with us! Are you starting to see how amazing He is? Even as I am writing this, the Spirit is opening my eyes to ways I have limited His voice and presence in my life. Again, He is our guide, counselor, protector, and coach—we need Him actively involved in our lives!

In the next chapter, we will dive into what it means to be intimate with our awesome God.

GET TO KNOW THE SPIRIT

*I will ask the Father, and He will give you another Comforter
(Counselor, Helper, Intercessor, Advocate, Strengthener, and Standby),
that He may remain with you forever—The Spirit of Truth....*

—John 14:16-17 AMP

The Holy Spirit is truly amazing! Next to our salvation through Christ, He is the best gift we will ever receive. Who is the Holy Spirit? Seasoned author and lifelong pastor A.W. Tozer shares...

> "The Holy Spirit is not enthusiasm...He is a Person. Put that down in capital letters—that the Holy Spirit is not only a Being having another mode of existence, but He is Himself a Person, with all the qualities and powers of personality. He is not matter, but He is substance.... The Holy Spirit has will and intelligence and feeling and knowledge and sympathy and ability to love and see and think and hear and speak and desire the same as any person has."[1]

Before you began this study, who did you understand the Holy Spirit to be? How has this chapter expanded your understanding of who He is to you personally?

_____

_____

_____

_____

Carefully meditate on the list of names used for the Holy Spirit in Scripture (see page 17). What do these names show you about who He is?

_____

_____

_____

_____

Knowing that the Holy Spirit is a Person equal to the Father and the Son is vital to developing a healthy relationship with God. Tozer continues…

> "…All that the Son is the Holy Ghost is, and all that the Father is the Holy Ghost is, and the Holy Ghost is in His Church. What will we find Him to be like? He will be exactly like Jesus. You have read your New Testament, and you know what Jesus is like, and the Holy Spirit is exactly like Jesus, for Jesus was God and the Spirit is God, and the Father is exactly like the Son; and you can know what Jesus is like by knowing what the Father is like, and you can know what the Spirit is like by knowing what Jesus is like."[2]

Are you seeing the Holy Spirit in a new way? How do these different facets of His character encourage you and motivate you to involve Him more in your life?

For Further Study…
John 12:44-45; 14:8-11; 2 Corinthians 4:4; Colossians 1:15-19; Hebrews 1:3.

HE IS DEITY, NOT AN ENTITY

*The Lord and the Spirit are **one and the same**....*

—2 Corinthians 3:17 CEV

As God's child, you have been given His precious, promised gift: the gift of His Holy Spirit (see Galatians 4:6). His Spirit is not just a mystical power or force that moves throughout the galaxy. His Holy Spirit is *Him*—the fullness of who He is, nothing held back.

Andrew Murray, nineteenth century minister and author of over 200 books, said that the Holy Spirit is "one with the Father and the Son" and that He brings "the full and perfect revelation" of God's glory. He continues:

> "All that in the Old Covenant had been promised by God, all that had been manifested and brought nigh to us of Divine grace in Jesus, **the Holy Spirit** is now to make our very own. *Through Him all the promises of God are fulfilled, all grace and salvation in Christ become a personal possession and experience.*"[3]

Did you catch that? Through the Holy Spirit, all God's promises are fulfilled and become a personal possession and experience. This is not just one man's opinion; it's the truth of Scripture. Carefully read and meditate on these passages.

> May blessing (praise, laudation, and eulogy) be to the God and Father of our Lord Jesus Christ (the Messiah) Who has blessed us in Christ with *every spiritual* (given by the Holy Spirit) *blessing* in the heavenly realm!
>
> —Ephesians 1:3 AMP

> *Everything* that goes into a life of pleasing God has been miraculously given to us by getting to know, personally and intimately, the One who invited us to God [the Holy Spirit]. The best invitation we ever received!
>
> —2 Peter 1:3 The Message
> {Words in brackets added for clarity.}

But as it is written: "Eye has not seen, nor ear heard, nor have entered into the heart of man the things which God has prepared for those who love him". But God has, *through the Spirit*, let us share his secret. For nothing is hidden from the Spirit, not even the deep wisdom of God.

—1 Corinthians 2:9-10 J.B. Phillips

What is the Holy Spirit revealing to you through these verses?

_____

_____

_____

Are you limiting the Holy Spirit's presence and power in your life by your perception of who He is? *Pause and pray.* Ask Him to show you where you may need Him to change your perspective. Write what He reveals.

_____

_____

_____

_____

For Further Study...
Do an online search of the phrases "by the Spirit," "through the Spirit," and "from the Spirit" (www.biblia.com). Also consider 1 Corinthians 12:4-11; Galatians 5:5; 2 Thessalonians 2:13.

HE IS THE *SPIRIT OF LIFE*

For the law of the Spirit of life in Christ Jesus has
set you free from the law of sin and of death.

—Romans 8:2 NASB

The Holy Spirit is the Spirit of life! Wow, what a name! Think about it. Life is *everything*. It encompasses all aspects of health, growth, freshness, energy, vim, and vigor. There is no shadow of death operating in the Spirit of life— no sickness or disease, no weariness or fatigue, no staleness or decay—no form of death whatsoever.

The Spirit of life was present at the time of creation, breathing life into every area of the earth. International missionary and evangelist **Lester Sumrall** confirms this, stating,

> "The first place in recorded Scripture where we see activity of the Holy Spirit is in Genesis 1:2. It is remarkable that the first page and second verse of the Bible shows the activity of the Holy Spirit. ...It was the act of bringing cosmos, *beauty*, and loveliness out of chaos. The earth was without form and void. God was involved in His creative masterpiece, and the Holy Spirit moved to help Him. The Spirit of God moved on the face of the waters, and *cosmos came out of the chaos*."[4]

Where in your life do you sense a void or see chaos? Where do you need the Holy Spirit of life to bring *beauty, order,* and *freedom*? Pray and ask Him to show you. Surrender these areas to Him in prayer, asking Him to move over them and bring order, just as He did at creation.

_____

_____

_____

_____

_____

Check out Philippians 4:6-8; 1 Peter 5:7; Psalm 37:4-6.

Are you worn out from the busyness of routine? The Spirit of life wants to strengthen you with His might. As you spend time with Him and get to know Him, He will renew your strength. Take a moment and meditate on these powerful promises from God:

> Have you not known? Have you not heard? The everlasting God, the Lord, the Creator of the ends of the earth, does not faint or grow weary; there is no searching of His understanding. He gives power to the faint and weary, and to him who has no might He increases strength [causing it to multiply and making it to abound].
> —Isaiah 40:28-29 AMP

> It stands to reason, doesn't it, that if the alive-and-present God who raised Jesus from the dead moves into your life, he'll do the same thing in you that he did in Jesus, bringing you alive to himself? When God lives and breathes in you (and he does, as surely as he did in Jesus), you are delivered from that dead life. With his Spirit living in you, your body will be as alive as Christ's!
> —Romans 8:11 The Message

> I have strength for all things in Christ Who empowers me [I am ready for anything and equal to anything through Him Who infuses inner strength into me...].
> —Philippians 4:13 AMP

What is the Holy Spirit speaking to you through these verses? **Write a prayer** asking the Spirit of life to *infuse you with inner strength* and make you as alive as Jesus when He walked the earth.

For Further Study...
Genesis 1:2; Nehemiah 9:6; Isaiah 40:12-15; Psalm 8:3-9; 104:24-30; Job 33:4

WE MUST TOTALLY *DEPEND* ON HIM

...You won't succeed by might or by power, but by my Spirit,
says the LORD of Armies.

—Zechariah 4:6 GW

Jesus Christ, the Son of God, was totally dependent on the Holy Spirit, the Spirit of the Father. Everything about Him, from His conception to His resurrection, was a result of the Spirit's work. Scripture says...

He was *conceived by the Spirit* – **Matthew 1:20; Luke 1:31-35**.

He was *led by the Spirit* – **Matthew 4:1; Luke 4:1**.

He was *empowered by the Spirit* – **Luke 4:14, 18-19; John 3:34**.

He was *taught by the Spirit* and obeyed Him – **John 5:19-20, 30; 14:10**.

Jesus said to the Jews, "I can guarantee this truth: The Son cannot do anything
on his own. He can do only what he sees the Father doing. Indeed,
the Son does exactly what the Father does. The Father loves the Son and
shows him everything he is doing.... I can't do anything on my own.
As I listen to the Father, I make my judgments. My judgments are right
because I don't try to do what I want but what the one who sent me wants."

—John 5:19-20, 30 GW

Carefully meditate on Jesus' declaration of dependence in John 5 (above). What is the Holy Spirit revealing to you about Jesus' relationship with Him? How does this challenge and motivate you?

Read Acts 5:32; Romans 8:16; Galatians 4:6; 1 John 3:24 and 4:13. What two recurring truths about the Holy Spirit and our relationship with Him can you identify?

_____

_____

_____

_____

Like the early believers at the church of Galatia, we sometimes forget just how much we need the Holy Spirit. Carefully read Galatians 3:2-9, along with Luke 11:13. What lessons about receiving the ongoing help of the Holy Spirit can you learn and apply in your own life?

_____

_____

_____

_____

HE'S YOUR *FOREVER FRIEND!*

I will talk to the Father, and he'll provide you another Friend so that you will always have someone with you. This Friend is the Spirit of Truth.

—John 14:16-17 The Message

The Holy Spirit wants to be your best friend! He wants to be your side-by-side, forever Helper twenty-four/seven. Scripture declares, "The Spirit Whom He has caused to dwell in us yearns over us and He yearns for the Spirit [to be welcome] with a jealous love" (James 4:5 AMP).

True friendship with the Holy Spirit is priceless. His presence and power provide everlasting satisfaction that is unsurpassed. Speaking of the Holy Spirit, Jesus said, "but those who drink the water that I will give them will never be thirsty again. The water that I will give them will become in them a spring which will provide them with life-giving water and give them eternal life" (John 4:14 GNT). Expounding on this verse, evangelist and educator **R.A. Torrey** stated,

> "Water here means the Holy Spirit. The world can never satisfy. Of every worldly joy it must be said: 'Whosoever drinketh of this water shall thirst again.' But *the Holy Spirit has power to satisfy every longing of the soul.* The Holy Spirit and He alone can satisfy the human heart.
>
> If you give yourself up to the Holy Spirit's inflowing or upspringing in your heart, you will never thirst. Oh, with what joy unutterable and satisfaction indescribable the Holy Spirit has poured forth His living water in many souls. Have you this living fountain within? Is the spring unchoked? Is it springing up into everlasting life?"[5]

Ponder the question presented by Torrey: "Have I this living fountain within? Am I experiencing the indescribable satisfaction of the Spirit? If not, why?" Then ask the Holy Spirit to show you what you can do to daily and more freely abandon yourself to His friendship. Write what He reveals.

Get quiet before the Lord (who is the Holy Spirit). Ask Him to make Himself real to you—more real than ever before. Ask Him to shower you with His love, acceptance, and peace. Don't rush. Be still and know by experience that He is God. Write anything He speaks to you.

_____

_____

_____

_____

You're free to be yourself with the Holy Spirit. He knows you inside and out. When you can't seem to "find yourself," He can tell you exactly where you are. He permanently abides in you to strengthen, encourage, and guide. Go to Him anytime, anywhere. You cannot weary Him or wear out your welcome. He is your best friend!

_____

_____

_____

Prayer
Holy Spirit, radically expand my understanding of who You are. Help me see Your personality and role as my Helper like never before. Help me to never again limit Your presence, power, or voice in my life. I pray this for myself, my family, and Your entire Church. In Jesus' name, Amen.

DISCUSSION QUESTIONS

If you are using this book as part of the Messenger Series on the Holy Spirit, please refer to video session 1.

1 | Our Christian life *without* the Holy Spirit becomes dry, monotonous, and powerless. So what should our lives be like *with* the Holy Spirit? Name as many positive manifestations and aspects as you can think of.

> *For the Lord is the Spirit, and wherever the Spirit of the Lord is, there is freedom.*
>
> —2 Corinthians 3:17 NLT

2 | The Holy Spirit is not an "it" or a divine, mystical power. He is the Person of the Godhead who carries the *fullness* of God the Father and the Son. What are some of the consequences of seeing the Holy Spirit as just an "it" or mystical power? What are the positive results of seeing Him as He really is: fully God?

3 | The involvement of the Holy Spirit was common among early believers, but it is rarer among believers today. What do you think are some reasons we have drawn back from enjoying, seeking out, and depending on the leadership and powerful influence of the Spirit of God?

4 | Where is the Person of Jesus right now? As a believer, is He living in your heart? What is a better, more accurate way of describing our salvation experience and the mystery of how God makes your heart His home?

Leaders: Have your class check out Mark 16:19; Acts 1:9-11; 7:55-56; Romans 8:34; Colossians 3:1; Hebrews 10:12-13 for the first part of question and Romans 8:9-10; 1 Corinthians 3:16; 6:19; 1 John 3:24 for the remainder.

> *Jesus answered and said to him, "If anyone loves Me,*
> *he will keep My word; and My Father will love him, and*
> *We will come to him and make Our home with him."*

> —John 14:23

5 | The Lord our God is One, and yet He has three distinct expressions—
Father, *Son*, and *Holy Spirit*. Describe the major functions of each
member of the Godhead and how they work together to accomplish
God's will.

> **Leaders:** Have your class check out 1 Corinthians 12:5-7 plus the account of creation in
> Genesis 1 and Jesus' words in John 5:17, 19-20.

The Spirit of God the Father = the Spirit of Christ = the Holy Spirit

6 | Jesus said the Holy Spirit is our Helper—our *parakletos*. This means
He is *"permanently* called alongside us to coach and counsel us in our
daily walk with God." In what ways does this knowledge motivate and
encourage you in your daily relationship with Him?

7 | What new characteristics of the Person of the Holy Spirit do you now
see that you didn't see before? How has this opened your eyes and
enriched your understanding of who He is in your life?

NOTES

CHAPTER SUMMARY:

- The **Holy Spirit** is a member of the Godhead who carries the fullness of God the Father and the Son.

- He is not an "it" or a mystical power; He is God.

- He is not limited by time or space; He can communicate with and assist an unlimited number of people all at the same time.

- He was intimately involved in the lives of early believers, and He yearns to be involved in every area of our lives today.

- There is virtually no Christian life without Him, but there is an abundant life of adventure to those who embrace His awesome fellowship.

- Get to know Him personally!

2

The Personality of the Holy Spirit

*The amazing grace of the Master, Jesus Christ, the extravagant love of God, the **intimate friendship of the Holy Spirit**, be with all of you.*

—2 Corinthians 13:14 The Message

Day 1

In order for us to enter into a close relationship with another person, we must first seek to understand what makes that individual tick. A greater knowledge of a person's likes, dislikes, aims, and ambitions will help develop a deeper friendship. Likewise, if we are to be intimate with the Holy Spirit, we must first seek to understand His personality.

As we discovered in the last chapter, Jesus made this astounding statement to His disciples: "It is to your advantage that I go away; for if I do not go away, the Helper will not come to you; but if I depart, I will send Him to you" (John 16:7). This is the same Jesus who once said, "I will open My mouth in parables; I will utter things that have been hidden since the foundation of the world" (Matthew 13:35 AMP). Jesus, the greatest teacher who ever lived, the One who revealed mysteries that had been hidden since the foundation of the world, is attempting to convince His closest followers that the Spirit of God—not Jesus Himself physically present—would be the best companion for them and the generations of believers to come. Wow! I don't know about you, but this makes me want to know more about the Holy Spirit.

Let's start by taking a look at 2 Corinthians 13:14. Paul states:

> The grace of the Lord Jesus Christ, and the love of God, and the communion of the Holy Spirit be with you all.

Paul highlights what stands out about each person of the Godhead. He starts with "the grace of the Lord Jesus Christ..." As believers, we must never forget that our right standing with God—which is the very cornerstone of this amazing relationship with the Spirit—would have never been possible if it were not for the grace of our Lord and Savior, Jesus Christ. This grace cannot be earned or merited; it is the great gift of His life, which includes forgiveness, redemption, and empowerment.

Paul goes on to say, "...and the love of God..." When I think of how much I love my four sons, I can't imagine life with only one of them. However, if I imagine only having one of my boys, and then consider giving him to die for my enemies—that thought is incomprehensible. Yet we were God's enemies when He freely gave His only Son for us (see Romans 5:10). What amazing love! Aren't you glad the Father loves you? Though you were His enemy, you're now His child; therefore how much more will He lavish His love upon you. He loves you uniquely and completely as His very own.

I absolutely adore my children, yet my ability to love and delight in them isn't even close to God's love for us. His Word declares, "Neither death nor life, nor angels nor principalities nor powers, nor things present nor things to come, nor height nor depth, nor any other created thing, shall be able to separate us from the love of God which is in Christ Jesus our Lord" (Romans 8:38-39). What an amazing promise! Aren't you thankful that nothing can separate you from the Father's love?

Now, let's look at the last portion of 2 Corinthians 13:14, keeping in mind that this is Paul's final letter to the Corinthians. This book (originally a letter) is packed with extraordinary wisdom and revelation. What does Paul, by the Spirit's leading, choose as the conclusion of this profound written correspondence? "The communion of the Holy Spirit be with you all." Notice that Paul associates the word *communion* with the Holy Spirit. As someone who grew up in the Catholic Church, when I used to see the word *communion*, I would think of bread and wine. Clearly, that is not what Paul is referring to. So, what does "communion with the Holy Spirit" mean? If we return to the original Greek, we find that the Greek word for *communion* is *koinonia*. Here are some definitions that I have found for this Greek word: *fellowship, companionship, communication, intimacy, sharing together, social intercourse, partnership, joint participation,* and *close mutual association.* That's a long, powerful list! Allow me to break it down into three main categories:

- Fellowship
- Partnership
- Intimacy

Communion Means Fellowship

My dictionary defines *fellowship* as "a friendly relationship, companionship, sharing together." Intimate friends or comrades experience fellowship. They share together, talk to each other, and stay aware of what's going on in each other's lives.

As I mentioned previously, I really enjoy playing golf. When I go play a round of golf, I am usually joined by some close friends. We spend the whole round talking with each other. It is one of the best environments for quality time because there are few distractions. I used to have a lot of fun playing tennis in college, but the problem with playing tennis was I couldn't talk with my opponent. One of the main reasons I love golf is that I get to converse with my competitors. I have developed more close relationships on a golf course than practically anywhere else. That's where my "fellowship" happens. Now you can probably understand why I *really* want my wife to play golf with me—because there is no person on the planet whose company I prefer to hers!

Likewise, some of my closest friends are members of the Messenger International team. We regularly discuss our intentions, challenges, and goals. I heavily rely on their expertise and friendship. I don't know where I would be today without these amazing men and women. We are continually engaged with each other; without this ongoing fellowship, Messenger International's mission to teach, reach, and rescue would not be possible.

It's evident in Scripture that the apostles completely depended on their fellowship with the Holy Spirit. In Acts we read, "And now I [Paul] am bound by the Spirit to go to Jerusalem. I don't know what awaits me, except that the Holy Spirit tells me in city after city that jail and suffering lie ahead" (Acts 20:22-23 NLT). Paul conversed with the Holy Spirit about what lay ahead of him. Notice the Holy Spirit didn't tell him that jail and suffering awaited him in *one* city. Rather, because of his regular fellowship with the Spirit, Paul knew that hardship awaited him in *city after city*.

I don't know about you, but if my partner—the one I am in close fellowship with—kept telling me that suffering awaited me everywhere I went, I would probably start questioning him. I would say things like, "Have you changed your mind?" or "Maybe this can be altered just a little bit," or "How about some minor inconveniences instead of suffering?" The Holy Spirit wasn't rejoicing in Paul's suffering but rather preparing Paul for what lay ahead, and He could do this because they were in close fellowship.

There have been times when the Holy Spirit has told me things I did not want to hear. I kept asking Him about these things (hoping for a different response), but I received the same message day after day. When we interact with the Spirit in this way, He eventually gets quiet. It's as if He is saying, "I have already made this abundantly clear to you; now you choose whether you are going to accept My direction." Being in close fellowship with the Holy Spirit means there will be times when He tells you things you simply don't want to hear.

In Acts 10 we find an account of Peter receiving this type of direction from the Holy Spirit. God gave Peter a vision that revealed God's willingness to extend salvation to the Gentiles. In verse 19, we read, "While Peter thought about the vision, the Spirit said to him, 'Behold, three men are seeking you.'" These men were coming to escort Peter to the home of a Gentile centurion—a place that Peter, as a devout Jewish man, would never have ordinarily gone. Therefore the Holy Spirit clearly told him, "Hey, you have some visitors down there, and I want you to go with them. I need you on this assignment." The Holy Spirit knew that Peter would not be overjoyed about this directive, but He gave the instruction without offering any further explanation.

A couple chapters earlier, we find another example of reliance on the Holy Spirit. "Now an *angel* of the Lord spoke to Philip, saying, 'Arise and go toward the south along the road which goes down from Jerusalem to Gaza'" (Acts 8:26). Here we find an angel of the Lord giving Philip a directive. It does not say an angel *appeared* to Philip; rather it says "an angel of the Lord *spoke* to Philip." Every single translation confirms this detail. Why is this distinction important? Through this passage we can deduce that Philip could discern between the voice of an angel and the voice of the Holy Spirit, because later in this same chapter we read, "The *Spirit* said to Philip, 'Go near and overtake this chariot'" (Acts 8:29). Philip was familiar with the Holy Spirit's voice, even to the point that he could distinguish between the voice of the Spirit and the voice of an angel!

I have come to know the voice of my wife so distinctly I can identify it anywhere, even if I'm not looking at her. We might be separated in a room full of people, but when she speaks, I will recognize her voice over the dozens of other voices in the room. This was how well the early believers knew the Spirit's voice. I can imagine Philip telling this story to Luke as he wrote the book of Acts. Perhaps Philip said, "No, Luke, it was not the Spirit who spoke to me in the city. It was an angel. But it was the Spirit who told me to join the chariot." Are we that familiar with His voice? Or could it be there is a greater closeness with the Spirit we have not yet entered?

When Philip was in the desert, the Holy Spirit told him to overtake a certain chariot. Why was this encounter significant? The gentleman in the chariot was third in command over all of Ethiopia. Because of his authority and influence, the Ethiopian's salvation was the beginning of the gospel's advancement in his nation. If Philip had not been sensitive to the Spirit's leading, he would have missed a great opportunity.

Several chapters later, we find another account involving Timothy, Paul, and Silas:

Now when they [Timothy, Paul, and Silas] had gone through Phrygia and the region of Galatia, they were forbidden by the Holy Spirit to preach the word in Asia. After they had come to Mysia, they tried to go into Bithynia, but the Spirit did not permit them. (Acts 16:6-7)

Notice it says that they were "forbidden" by the Holy Spirit and that "the Spirit did not permit them."

Are you starting to see how much communication occurred between the early believers and the Holy Spirit? Should it be any different today? Do we have better ways of serving God apart from the Holy Spirit? Were the early Church leaders simply primitive in their methods because they lacked modern technology? Absolutely not. No technology or method could ever take the place of the Holy Spirit's voice. These leaders expected the Spirit to be intimately involved in their lives, and they respected and invited His presence. Nothing has changed. The Spirit desires to walk in equally close fellowship with us today.

Can you imagine Lisa and me spending every hour of every day together in our house without saying one word to each other? That would be ridiculous. Who would ever want a marriage like that? I love my wife and desire to be close to her. I love hearing from her; the sound of her voice is music to my ears. We've been married for over thirty years, but if she were single (thank God she isn't), I would be hot on her trail. Out of every person on the planet, she is without a doubt the one I most desire to be with. In the same way, the Holy Spirit desires to be in close fellowship with you.

I have been staying in hotel rooms for twenty-four years and I've never been bored. How could I ever be bored when I'm with God every moment? He's in my room with me. For this reason, I am protective of my time in hotel rooms. Periodically I'll say, "I don't want to spend time with my travel team because I want to be alone with the Holy Spirit." I love to hear Him speak. Don't get me wrong, I like being around people; in fact, I like it a lot! In no way am I a hermit or recluse. I absolutely love people, but I really value my time (fellowship) with the Holy Spirit.

Communion Means Partnership

The next English word that can be used to describe *koinonia* is *partnership*. We see an example of partnership in the Gospel of Luke: "And when they had done this, they caught a great number of fish, and their net was breaking. So they signaled to their *partners* in the other boat to come and help them. And they came and filled both the boats, so that they began to sink" (Luke 5:6-7). The Greek word for *partners* is *metochos* (a synonym of *koinonia*) and is defined as "'partner, companion, fellow worker."[1] These men were business partners. From this interaction, we understand that good partnership requires both communication and action. The men had to signal to their partners, and then the partners had to come and help.

Now let's look at what is probably one of the most awe-inspiring scriptures in the whole New Testament. Paul writes, "We are labourers together with God" (1 Corinthians 3:9 KJV). Isn't that amazing? I like the way the Weymouth translation puts it: "[We are] fellow workers *for* and *with* God." We have been given the opportunity to work *for* and *with* the Creator of the heavens and the earth. Another way to put this is we get to work *in partnership with God*. What an amazing invitation!

Effective partners develop ebb and flow with each other. I grew up near Lake Michigan, and sailing was a big part of my life. I enjoyed our family's sailboat, took two years of sailing school, and even raced competitively. On one of my first races, I was asked to work with a great captain whose crew was one of the best. They were excited for me to join the team. During our first race, I felt like the odd man out. The captain issued orders and the crew flew into action. Each man knew exactly what he was to do and took his station on the boat. On the other hand,

I was quite awkward. Though I had been told what to do, I had not developed in my role. The other crewmembers had established a rhythm of collaboration that I had yet to learn.

Partnering with the Holy Spirit is like being part of that crew. You must work with Him. The first time I preached publicly, my wife and her best friend fell asleep on the front row. I wasn't working with the ebb and flow of the Spirit. It took some time, but I discovered how to partner with Him when I speak. The same thing occurred with writing. I took a full, frustrated year on the first book I wrote as I learned to work in partnership with Him. Eventually writing became much easier and faster. I've learned that in both these things, He has a role and so do I—and He wants it that way!

In Acts 15 we see an element of partnership in action. The apostles were constructing a letter to be sent to all the Gentile believers. In it, they said, "It seemed good to the Holy Spirit, and to us" (Acts 15:28). We can see the partnership at work. The leaders distinctly expressed both the Holy Spirit's views and their own regarding a particular situation. Both parties participated in the decision. Both parties had a role. They were partners in the kingdom work.

This same idea of partnership is also seen in the Old Testament. Remember when God came to Abraham at the terebinth trees to discuss His plans to destroy Sodom and Gomorrah (see Genesis 18). God clearly sees Abraham as His partner. God and Abraham walk over to a cliff and God says, "I'm really considering blowing up these two cities. What do you think, Abraham?" (author's paraphrase). Abraham is quite concerned because his nephew lives in one of these two cities. After considerable deliberations he eventually convinces God not to destroy the cities if ten righteous people can be found within them.

God clearly valued Abraham's input. He actually says in Genesis

18:17, "Shall I hide from Abraham what I am doing?" It is clear that God wanted to bring Abraham up to speed on His plans. Why? Because Abraham was in close communion or *partnership* with God.

A similar instance is found in the life of Moses. God said to Moses, "Let Me alone, that My wrath may burn hot against them [the children of Israel] and I may consume them. And I will make of you a great nation" (Exodus 32:10). After hearing this Moses proceeded to convince God to relent of His anger and change His plans. It's easy for us to read this today and make light of what transpired. But stop and think about this: Moses was able to remind God what was best for both Him and His people, even after God said, "Let Me alone!" This was because Moses worked in close partnership with God.

At this point, it is important for us to recognize that God is the Almighty and always deserves our reverence. It is only by His grace and power that we are able to partner with Him. He has chosen to allow us to be a part of His grand plan and design. But what a privilege He has given us through that choice!

These are two great accounts from the Old Testament, but the fact is that Abraham and Moses didn't have what we have today. There were specific moments and occasions when these giants of faith were able to partner with God in this way. However, the Holy Spirit lives within us twenty-four/seven. We don't have to wait for Him to visit us at the terebinth trees or climb the physical mountain of Sinai to interact with Him. We have access to Him at all times. And best of all, He desires to work in partnership with us—to direct our steps and hear our thoughts.

Not only is the Spirit with us at all times, but He also never has to sleep. Recently, I was up at 2:20 a.m. and couldn't go back to bed because I was excited about a day of ministry. So I got up and talked to my Partner. Guess what? He was awake. It was amazing! He didn't say, "John, why did you wake Me up?" On the other hand, my wife would have said, "John, why in the world are you waking me up so early in the morning?" If I responded with, "I just want to talk to you, babe," she would probably have hit me with a pillow. She really likes her sleep, so I know not to wake her up (and she knows the same of me when circumstances are reversed). But the Holy Spirit welcomes my company at any hour. He is excited to talk with me about the upcoming day, and sometimes He will even give me glimpses of what's going to happen. This is why I like to start every day in His presence. He is my Partner, and our communion is a vital part of my day.

It is important to note that the Holy Spirit is the senior Partner in this relationship. Paul said to the leaders at Ephesus, "Therefore take heed to yourselves and to all the flock, among which the *Holy Spirit has made you overseers*, to shepherd the church of *God* which He purchased with His own blood" (Acts 20:28). Notice Paul did not say "the flock, among which Jesus has made you overseers." This verse perfectly illustrates Jesus' partnership with the Holy Spirit. Jesus purchased the Church of God "with His own blood." The Holy Spirit, as the member of the Godhead currently residing on the earth, now appoints the Church's overseers and manages its affairs. He's in charge—or put another way, He is the senior Partner. Paul was very aware of the fact that the Holy Spirit is the One who resides with and in us.

Another example of this can be found in Acts 13: "As they ministered to the Lord and fasted, the *Holy Spirit* said, 'Now separate to Me Barnabas and Saul for the work to which I have called them." ...So, being sent out by the *Holy Spirit*, they went down to Seleucia" (verses 2 and 4). Again, in this instance we see the Holy Spirit clearly identified as the One who was partnering (in communion) with the apostles. Remember, Jesus is with His Father in heaven. The Holy Spirit has been sent to earth to partner with us in this amazing life.

Close Mutual Association

Let's look once again at 2 Corinthians 13:14: "The grace of the Lord Jesus Christ, and the love of God, and the communion of the Holy Spirit be with you all." Now that we've defined *communion* as "fellowship" and "partnership," see this verse through your new understanding of these two terms. Are you starting to realize the magnitude of Paul's statement? But it doesn't stop there. The word *koinonia* also conveys "close mutual association."

I'm going to give away my age with this comment, but when I think of *close mutual association*, I think of the Beatles. As a young boy (long before the Beatles ever separated), when someone said "Paul McCartney," I would immediately think of the other Beatles: John Lennon, George Harrison, and Ringo Starr. At that time I didn't even think of the Beatles as individuals; they were simply *the Beatles.*

Another example of close mutual association is the Three Stooges. They wouldn't be "three stooges" without Moe, Larry, *and* Curly—all three of them. An episode that only had Moe in it would be pretty ridiculous. What made the Three Stooges great was the dynamic of the three of them together. They were dependent on each other.

When I think of people who walk in close mutual association with the Holy Spirit, Dr. David Yonggi Cho is one of the first who comes to mind. Doctor Cho pastors one of the largest churches in the world. I'll never forget when I first met him in the 1980s. It was his first visit to my home church, and my role on our church staff gave me the opportunity to welcome and host our guest speakers. I had been doing this for several years by the time I met Dr. Cho, so by then I had probably hosted several dozen ministers. However, my encounter with Dr. Cho was completely unique. When he got into my car, the presence of the

Lord came with him. Almost immediately I started crying; tears were streaming down my face. I tried to remain silent, as I didn't want to disturb him before a time of ministry, but I eventually felt compelled to speak. I softly and soberly said, "Dr. Cho, God is here in our car." He smiled and nodded. "I know." This encounter makes sense to me when I consider how much Dr. Cho has written and preached about his communion with the Holy Spirit. I have heard him say that he prays for two to four hours a day, mostly in the Spirit. Dr. Cho makes quality time with the Holy Spirit a priority; for this reason God's presence is strong in his life.

Several years ago I preached about the Holy Spirit during the Sunday morning service at a large church. That night, when we returned for the evening service, I was supposed to start teaching around forty-five minutes after worship began. Instead, the Holy Spirit began moving and people were being healed and saved. I didn't get the microphone for two hours. Finally, before I was given the platform, the pastor (who is no soft or weak man) came to me in tears saying, "John, in the eight years that I have led this church, I have never felt the presence of God so strongly!" I immediately replied, "There is a reason for that. It's because we talked about the Holy Spirit this morning, and whenever you talk about Him, He will manifest." This perfectly illustrates what will happen when you and I, as "ordinary" believers, walk in close mutual association with the Spirit.

Communion Means Intimacy

The final meaning of *koinonia* is "intimacy." This is actually the word that best describes Paul's use of *koinonia* in 2 Corinthians 13:14. Intimacy can only be developed through fellowship or relationship, but it goes beyond the connotation of both these terms. Intimacy goes deep into the thoughts, secrets, and desires of the heart.

In *The Message* version of the Bible, we read, "The intimate friendship of the Holy Spirit, be with all of you" (2 Corinthians 13:14). I look at intimacy as the deepest level of friendship. Never forget that the Holy Spirit's desire is to be your friend; He yearns for your fellowship. James 4:5 says, "The Spirit who dwells in us yearns jealously." He is jealous for you and longs for your time and attention. Just think: the Holy Spirit is God, and nothing is hidden from Him. His knowledge, wisdom, and understanding are limitless—and He longs to reveal Himself to you. When I know or understand something of great value or importance, I passionately desire to share it with those who are close to me. The same is probably true of you, and the Holy Spirit is no different.

Too often, believers attempt to draw close to Jesus outside of relationship with the Holy Spirit. This is similar to the mistake that the Pharisees made. They said to Jesus, "'We are not illegitimate children... The only Father we have is God himself.' Jesus said to them, 'If God were your Father, you would love me, for I have come here from God. I have not come on my own; God sent me'" (John 8:41-42 NIV). The Pharisees wanted a relationship with the Father apart from Jesus. They were unwilling to accept that God had something different in mind. Jesus explained to the Pharisees that He and His Father are one. In fact, He later said, "If you really know me, you will know my Father as well" (John 14:7 NIV). But the Pharisees simply refused to listen. Because they were unwilling to come to the Father through the Son, they could not truly be close to the Father at all.

In the same way, Jesus made it clear that He is no longer on the earth and that the Father sent the Holy Spirit (One who is just like our Savior) to be our Helper (John 16:7). The Spirit has been sent to reveal Jesus, just as the Son was sent to reveal the Father. We must remember that the Holy Spirit loves to glorify Jesus. So if you really want to know more about Jesus, you must spend time with the Holy Spirit. The Spirit will clearly reveal Jesus to you. But the Holy Spirit will only manifest where He is honored. As we honor the Spirit, He will reveal Himself to us, and we will enjoy both His amazing presence and a greater awareness of the One He reveals.

Over the last thirty years of ministry, I have never seen an exception to this truth: the people who know Jesus the best are those who are most intimate with the Holy Spirit. This makes complete sense because the Spirit is the One who reveals Jesus to us.

Understanding the Spirit's Personality

In order to be intimate with someone, we must seek to know the personality of the one we desire intimacy with. This understanding will naturally enhance our communion and bring our intimacy to deeper levels.

For the longest time I treated all four of my boys the same way. This naturally caused some issues. Why was this form of parenting ineffective? Because each of my sons has a unique personality. My wife was sensitive to this and trained me in how to learn the differences between them. Seeking to understand the uniqueness of each of my sons has greatly enhanced my relationships with them.

Because I am very intimate with my wife, I am able to understand how she expresses herself. We have developed this intimacy because we've been married for over thirty years, and intimacy is a product of quality time. Lisa could give me one look, and I could write pages about what she is thinking. There are other times when I can tell you what Lisa wants without her saying a word to me. If you were to tell me,

"John, I'm serving bacon, eggs, and grits this morning," I could confidently respond, "You know what, Lisa will not want grits or bacon." I would not need to ask her; I already know that she doesn't like grits and bacon. This is a very superficial example, but the same is true about more personal matters. This type of intimacy didn't happen overnight. It had to be cultivated over years of quality time and communication. No one knows my wife's likes and dislikes better than I do, and no one knows my likes and dislikes better than my wife does. In the same way, we grow in our understanding of the Holy Spirit as we make a commitment to communicate with Him and spend time in His presence.

Day 4

Knowing His Nature

In John chapters 14 through 16, Jesus uses the pronouns *He, Him,* and *Himself* nineteen times in reference to the Holy Spirit. It is very evident that the Holy Spirit is a Person. Again, by calling Him a Person I am not calling Him human. Remember, human beings were created in God's likeness. This means that aspects of what we consider "personality" reflect what first exists in God, but God is not an exact likeness of us. Therefore, there are facets of His Person that will never fit into our proverbial human "boxes."

There is a discovery I have made that really helps me in how I relate to and interact with the Holy Spirit. As I studied the pronouns used for the Holy Spirit in the original Greek, I noticed that the Greek pronoun often used for the Holy Spirit is a gender-neutral pronoun (it is not explicitly male or female). In fact, it can be used for either male or female while describing only one person.

We do not have this type of pronoun in our English language. We have *he, she,* and *it. It* is a pronoun for an object or an animal. *He* refers to a male, and *she* refers to a female. There is no singular, gender-neutral pronoun to describe a male or female. But such a gender-neutral pronoun *does* exist in the Greek, and in the New Testament, you will find it used often in reference to the Holy Spirit. Again, this pronoun refers to a being, not an object.

In the Old Testament, you will find something similar. In the original Hebrew, there are many cases where the action assigned to the Holy Spirit is feminine by function (not feminine by form). The Hebrews often wrote according to function (according to what someone or something did, as opposed to who or what it was). Nowhere in Scripture is the Holy Spirit ever described as female, but some of His actions were assigned an attribute of femininity.

This is a deep topic that I do not have room to expound on here, but let me make one thing abundantly clear: I do not think the Holy Spirit is a female. In fact, let me write that again more directly: the Holy Spirit is not a female. Some people teach this doctrine, and I find it to be ungrounded and highly sensationalized. Please get that notion way out of your head. The Holy Spirit is not a goddess.

Here is what I am saying. We must remember that God was not created in our image. We were created in His image. I know that sounds elementary, but this truth is of paramount importance as we continue in this study. In Genesis 1:27 we read, "God created *human beings* in his own image. In the image of God he created them; male and female" (NLT). Other translations say "God created man" or "mankind." Personally, I think "human beings" or "mankind" is the best translation. So in Genesis we learn that God created men and women *in His image.* The question has to be asked, if He created both male and female in His image, then doesn't this mean that the characteristics we might consider "feminine" must have their origin in God? Is it possible that the being of the Holy Spirit supersedes or transcends our understanding of male or female? It must be, for both men and women were created in the image of God.

I am sure you have noticed that I have referred to the Holy Spirit as "He," "Him," or "Himself" throughout this book, and I will continue to do so. This concept—of the Holy Spirit's having attributes that we categorize as feminine—can be complex and confusing for English-speaking people. So why am I writing on this? I wouldn't include this topic if I didn't think it could improve your understanding of and relationship with the Holy Spirit.

He Is Tender and Gentle

Let me tell you a little more about my background before I continue. My father is a World War II veteran. He is ninety-three years old, and I love him dearly. My dad taught me many things that have greatly benefitted me over the course of my life. However, one thing that he did not prepare me for was how to be married to a woman. Peter once said, "Treat your wife with understanding as you live together" (1 Peter 3:7 NLT). When I married Lisa, I did not treat her "with understanding." Lisa was the first love of my life. I had not been in intimate friendship with another woman before her. So I treated her like one of the guys. As you can imagine, this approach was not successful. I had to learn how to interact with her *as a woman*.

One thing I had to learn was how to speak to Lisa with gentleness. Unfortunately, there have been times when I have communicated roughly with members of my family. Thankfully, the Holy Spirit convicts me, and then I am able to apologize and make things right. One time I really messed up with one of my sons, and I had to go to him and apologize.

He was quick to forgive me, and everything was great between us. With Lisa, it was a different story. She was upset with me for a few days because of the harsh way I had spoken to my son. This wasn't an issue of offense; it is the natural byproduct of her sensitivity in relationships. My son and I reconciled almost immediately, but I had to put a little work into restoring my communion with my wife. Two days after the incident, she said to me, "I'm still reeling from the way you spoke to our son." I have learned that this is a gift in Lisa's life. Like many women, she is extremely relational and very protective of those who are close to her.

Could it be that the Holy Spirit also possesses this great relational strength that we typically consider to be feminine? The Bible says, "Do not grieve the Holy Spirit of God" (Ephesians 4:30). As Rick Renner points out in *Sparkling Gems from the Greek*, the word translated here as *grieve* conveys "deep sorrow and distress." It comes from a word denoting a pain that can only be experienced between two people who deeply love each other. So what Paul is essentially saying is, "Don't grievously hurt the One who deeply loves you." Now let's read this scripture in context:

> Don't use foul or abusive language. Let everything you say be good and helpful, so that your words will be an encouragement to those who hear them. And *do not bring sorrow* [grief] to God's Holy Spirit by the way you live. Remember, he has identified you as his own, guaranteeing that you will be saved on the day of redemption. Get rid of all bitterness, rage, anger, harsh words, and slander, as well as all types of evil behavior. Instead, be kind to each other, tenderhearted, forgiving one another, just as God through Christ has forgiven you. (Ephesians 4:29-32 NLT)

Are you seeing the tenderness of the Holy Spirit?

Tenderness is truly a strength to be admired. Paul charges us to be tenderhearted. If I want to enjoy a healthy, vibrant relationship with my wife, then I had better be tenderhearted and speak accordingly toward my sons. Likewise, in order for us to enjoy a healthy, vibrant relationship with the Holy Spirit, we must be sensitive to the things that bring Him sorrow. It's quite interesting that Paul identifies bringing deep sorrow to the Spirit with the following behavior: *foul or abusive language, rage, anger, harsh words,* and *slander.* It's very much the same as my wife being grieved by similar behavior. Again, is this not evidence that the Spirit possesses a great relational strength that we typically consider to be feminine?

Notice Paul doesn't say, "Don't grieve Jesus." Likewise, he doesn't say, "Don't grieve the Father." He specifically says, "Don't grieve the Spirit." The Holy Spirit has made our hearts His dwelling place. Everywhere we go, He goes; that is an intimate association. Therefore He is deeply affected by what we allow into our lives.

Consider this from a different angle. If someone cusses me out, it's no big deal. But if someone cusses my wife out, they're in big trouble. Jesus made a similar point when He said, "Anyone who speaks a word against the Son of Man [Jesus], it will be forgiven him; but whoever speaks against the Holy Spirit, it will not be forgiven him, either in this age or in the age to come" (Matthew 12:32). Isn't it interesting that God the Father (revealed through the Son who only spoke His Father's will) places His protection on the Holy Spirit? The Father didn't evoke this type of protection on how we relate to Jesus or Himself, but He did so with the Holy Spirit.

The relationship between the Father, the Son, and the Holy Spirit is a mystery that we may never fully understand. It is interesting to note this distinction in our relationship with the Holy Spirit. Our interaction with Him is to be treasured and protected. It is important for us to remember that we can cause Him sorrow, at times even deep sorrow. Why is this so important to your relationship with Him? Because the manifestation of His presence in your life will be thwarted if you lack understanding of how you should relate to Him.

Day 5

He Is Sensitive, Yet Strong

The Holy Spirit is called the Comforter, correct? Who do children typically run to when they get hurt? They run to their mothers. In view of this, several states have created policies that highlight the role of female officers in addressing juvenile crime. Hawaii has a policy that encourages a female officer to be the first to interact with a recently arrested juvenile. They have learned that these juveniles respond better to female officers. Women naturally exhibit an innate ability to comfort and console. Again, in making these statements, I am not saying the Holy Spirit is a woman.

In some ways, I liken the Holy Spirit to King David. Have you ever noticed how tender David was? How compassionate and sensitive he was? When Absalom died, he wept even though he was the one who instructed the army to end Absalom's rebellion (see 2 Samuel 19). On multiple occasions we find David weeping and writing songs. His relationship with Jonathan is one of the best accounts in all of Scripture of an intimate, close friendship. But never forget that David was a warrior, one who defeated a giant and killed thousands of men. He was the leader of the Mighty Men—quite possibly the greatest group of fighters in the history of Israel (see 2 Samuel 23). In one instance, David even planned to kill a man who refused to give water and food to his followers (see 1 Samuel 25). David was not a wimp; he was a warrior. Yet he was one who was tender and sensitive.

Let me remind you that the Holy Spirit is also called the Spirit of might (see Isaiah 11:2). He is all-powerful, and in no way is He weak or impotent. Yet at the same time, He's kindhearted and feels things deeply. He can be made sorrowful by our words or actions. What an amazing God!

Don't be alarmed if you are having a hard time grasping the full nature of His personality. We must always remember that His personality cannot be confined to our human understanding. However, He has promised to reveal Himself to us if we draw near to Him. What an invitation!

As I've mentioned before, there is no way I can fully describe the mystery and glory of the Holy Spirit (see 1 Corinthians 2:6-16). My aim is to simply introduce you to Him so you can begin to discover His greatness and enjoy His presence in your life.

Be Careful Not to Grieve Him

Recently I refrained from watching any television for a period of time. My communion with God was powerful as I immersed myself in prayer and the Word. During this time I walked into our living room where my boys were watching a movie. It wasn't a bad movie, but I walked in during a scene in which a man was killed. I immediately left the room. Because I had grown so sensitive to the Spirit during our times of communion, I could feel His sorrow at the images on the screen.

We must never forget that the Spirit has taken up permanent residence in us. When you walk into a movie, you are taking Him—the God of the universe who is holy and infinite in might—with you. He's always with you because He promised to never leave nor forsake you. But you will find that when you drag Him into situations that grieve Him, He will suddenly become quiet.

What should our response be when we have caused the Spirit sorrow? We should immediately ask for forgiveness, but it must be a deep, sincere apology. When I've grieved my wife, a quick "let's get it right" apology never works. Lisa can see right through it. She knows I just want to go on with life rather than sincerely address the issues that caused the breach in our fellowship. Lisa's desire is not to condemn me but to make sure there is nothing disingenuous or artificial about our fellowship. In the same way, the Spirit of God is jealous over us; He doesn't want superficial fellowship, but genuine intimacy.

Earlier in this chapter I referred to a time when I spoke harshly to one of my sons. For the next couple of days after this incident, the Holy Spirit continued to bring it to my attention in my prayer closet. This wasn't condemnation. It was an issue of communion. I didn't realize how deeply I had saddened Him, and the first couple of times I asked for forgiveness, it wasn't motivated by true godly sorrow. I was more concerned about just moving on. His continued, gentle prompting brought me to the place of true, deep, godly sorrow, which in turn led to the clearing of my soul (mind, will, and emotions).

Paul addressed the Corinthian church similarly after their disobedience caused a breach in their fellowship with God. He wrote (and as you read his words, keep in mind they are from the Spirit of God):

Just see what this godly sorrow produced in you! Such earnestness, such concern to clear yourselves, such indignation, such alarm, such longing to see me. (2 Corinthians 7:11 NLT)

Thank God that we are forgiven and cleansed by the blood of the Lamb. But while we believers are in right standing with God, we still have to reestablish communion with the Holy Spirit when we have saddened Him. Just as the Apostle Paul did with the Corinthians until they were truly sorry, so the Holy Spirit persists in convicting us because He is zealous for our genuine fellowship. The godly sorrow I experienced produced a genuine earnestness to clear things up and a longing in my soul to be reconnected in communion. Thank God that the Holy Spirit is quick to forgive!

Never forget: the Holy Spirit is gentle, compassionate, and comforting (qualities that we often attribute to women); but He is also mighty, powerful, and like a warrior (qualities that we often attribute to men). We must learn more and more about His personality if we are to experience intimacy with Him. We need to connect with Him on His terms. As we grow in understanding of who the Holy Spirit is, we can experience deeper communion with the Almighty.

Sometimes I try to talk golf with my wife. I'll say something like, "Babe, guess what? I shot a 68 today!" My boys will be thrilled and say, "Dad, go through every single shot with us!" My wife, on the other hand, will be more interested in the conversations I had with my companions on the course. That's what really excites her—the relationships. If I want to connect with Lisa on her level, then I need to talk about things that interest her. In the same way, we must discover what interests and pleases the Spirit of God. As we explore His greatness by reading the Word and spending quality time in His presence, He will faithfully reveal Himself to us.

YOU CAN HEAR GOD'S VOICE!

Whoever belongs to God hears what God says....

—John 8:47 NIV

Yes, you can hear God's voice! He is still speaking to His people today, and He is speaking to us through His precious Holy Spirit. In an effort to connect Christians in a deeper, more personal relationship with God, authors **Henry Blackaby** and **Claude King** share:

> "God clearly spoke to His people in Acts. He clearly speaks to us to-day. From Acts to the present, God has been speaking to His people *by the Holy Spirit.* ...Because He is always present in a believer, He can speak to you clearly at any time and in any way He chooses."[1]

Jesus declared that He is the Good Shepherd and we are His sheep who can hear and know His voice. Meditate on His words in John 10:3-5, 11, 14, 27. What is the Holy Spirit revealing to you?

_____

_____

_____

_____

One name given for the Holy Spirit is *the Spirit of truth.* Why is this? Blackaby continues:

> "...You and I cannot understand the truth of God unless the Holy Spirit of God reveals it. He is our Teacher. When He teaches you the Word of God, sit before Him and respond to Him. As you pray, watch to see how He uses the Word of God to confirm in your heart a word from God. Watch what He is doing around you in circumstances. The God who is speaking to you as you pray and the God who is speaking to you in the Scriptures is the God who is working around you. God speaks by the Holy Spirit through the Bible, prayer, circumstances, and the church to reveal Himself, His purposes, and His ways."[2]

So, what are some of the main things you can expect the Holy Spirit to reveal to you? Carefully read Jesus' words in John 14:26; 15:26 and 16:12-15 and identify five things the Spirit teaches.

_____

_____

_____

_____

What is the key to knowing God's voice? Blackaby and King continue:

> "...The key to knowing God's voice is not a formula. It is not a method you can follow. Knowing God's voice comes from an intimate love relationship with God. ...As God speaks and you respond, you will come to the point that you recognize His voice more and more clearly."[3]

Relationship is the key to knowing and hearing God's voice. Enoch, Noah, Abraham, and many others experienced this firsthand, and so can you. What principle in Amos 3:7; Daniel 2:22 and Psalm 25:14 is reflected in John 15:15; 1 Corinthians 2:9-10 and Ephesians 1:9? How does this encourage you as a "last-days" believer?

_____

_____

_____

_____

For examples, **check out** the lives of Enoch (Genesis 5:21-24), Noah (Genesis 6:9-18), Abraham (Genesis 18:16-22), and Peter (Acts 10:9-23).

HIS PRESENCE IS YOUR VITAL NEED

You have said, Seek My face [inquire for and require My presence as your vital need]. My heart says to You, Your face (Your presence), Lord, will I seek....

—Psalm 27:8 AMP

David was not your average man. He had *one thing* that burned within his heart—one craving that consumed his consciousness. He had a passion for God's presence. "The *one thing* I ask of the Lord," he said, "the thing I seek most—is to live in the house of the Lord all the days of my life, delighting in the Lord's perfections and meditating in his Temple" (Psalm 27:4 NLT).

Nothing—absolutely nothing—is more valuable than the abiding presence of God and having Him as our Partner. Since the Father and the Son are in heaven, the Holy Spirit has been positioned on earth to manifest God's presence in and through every believer. Nicholas Herman, better known as **Brother Lawrence**, learned to "practice the presence of God" and made it his mission to help others do the same. According to this seventeenth century monastic servant,

> "The most holy and necessary practice in our spiritual life is the presence of God. That means finding constant pleasure in His divine company, speaking humbly and lovingly with Him in all seasons, at every moment, without limiting the conversation in any way."[4]

Stop and think: *How vital is God's presence in my life? What would life be like without Him?* Imagine getting up tomorrow *without* the presence of the Holy Spirit. Review the list of His names and roles (see page 17). With renewed perspective, write how vital His presence is to you.

When and where are we to experience the Holy Spirit's presence?
Lawrence continues:

> "It isn't necessary that we stay in church in order to remain in God's presence. We can make our hearts personal chapels where we can enter anytime to talk to God privately. These conversations can be so loving and gentle, and anyone can have them. Is there any reason not to begin?"[5]

Without question, you need quality time in the Holy Spirit's presence—a time to totally focus your attention on Him. This includes things like time in His Word, talking and listening to Him, thanking Him and singing His praise, and just sitting silently. Stop and pray: "Holy Spirit, what should *my* devotional time with You look like at this season of my life?" Write what He reveals.

_____

_____

_____

_____

How can you practice God's presence? Brother Lawrence said, "Simply present yourself to God...and fix your attention on His presence. If your mind wanders at times, don't be upset, because being upset will only distract you more. Allow your will to recall your attention gently to God... *cultivate the holy habit of thinking of Him often.*"[6] Pause and pray: "Holy Spirit, what can I do to focus my attention more on You?" Listen for His answer and incorporate it in your life.

For Further Study...
Check out 1 Chronicles 16:9-11; Psalm 22:26; 105:3-4; Proverbs 8:17-18; Isaiah 55:1-3, 6; Jeremiah 29:11-13; Matthew 6:33; Hebrews 12:1-2.

HE WANTS TO BE CLOSE TO YOU

"Look! I have been standing at the door and I am constantly knocking.
If anyone hears me calling him and opens the door,
I will come in and fellowship with him and he with me."

—Revelation 3:20 TLB

God, through the Person of the Holy Spirit, wants to be closer to you than any other person on earth. He desires *intimacy*—the deepest level of relationship you can experience.

It's been said that having intimacy with God is like saying God can "in-to-me-see," and it's true. The Holy Spirit can go where no man can go—inside our souls and spirits. He's not limited by time or space. Not only does the Spirit search and know our hearts, but He also searches and knows God's heart, revealing His deep thoughts, secrets, and desires—so that we can "in-to-Him-see."

The secret [of the sweet, satisfying companionship] of the Lord have they
who fear (revere and worship) Him, and He will show them
His covenant and reveal to them its [deep, inner] meaning.

—Psalm 25:14 AMP

Again, the Holy Spirit is "the Spirit of truth" who guides us into *all truth*. Is there an aspect about *God* or *Jesus* or a passage of *Scripture* you want to understand? Pray and ask the Holy Spirit to show you its true, deep meaning and how it applies to you. Write what He reveals.

_____

_____

_____

_____

And Jesus explained to them what was said about himself in all the Scriptures,
beginning with the books of Moses and the writings of all the prophets.

—Luke 24:27 GNT

The Spirit not only reveals truth about Scripture, but also truth about *us* and the things in our lives.

Is there an area in *your life* you just don't understand? Do you explode in anger or become extremely fearful in certain situations for no apparent reason? The Holy Spirit knows why. Pause and pray: "Holy Spirit, what is the true, root reason I am acting this way? Give me Your eyes to see. What do I need You to change in me to overcome this in my life?" Write what He reveals.

_____

_____

_____

_____

Is there a *circumstance*, past or present, you don't understand? The Spirit understands. Pause and pray: "Holy Spirit, what's the truth about this situation? How do You see it? What are You trying to change in me, and how can I cooperate with You to see it happen?" Write what He reveals.

_____

_____

_____

_____

For Further Study...
Jesus had intimacy with the Father: Matthew 14:22-23; 17:1-5; Mark 1:35; 6:31, 46-47; Luke 5:16; 6:12
God's Spirit is near to us as we draw near: Psalm 16:8; 34:18; 73:28; 145:18; Hebrews 10:22; James 4:8

BE CAREFUL NOT TO GRIEVE HIM

And do not bring sorrow to God's Holy Spirit by the way you live.
Remember, he has identified you as his own....

—Ephesians 4:30 NLT

Fellowship with the Holy Spirit is priceless! His manifest presence is life-giving in every area of living. For **Kathryn Kuhlman**, this was a way of life. Millions heard her speak about God's love and the power of His Spirit, many experiencing His miraculous healing. In her book, *The Greatest Power in the World*, Kuhlman explains how the Spirit can be grieved:

> "...Even though the Holy Spirit is the mighty power of the Trinity, He is *sensitive* and easily grieved. There is no doubt that this wonderful person may be grieved by bitterness, by wrath, anger, evil speaking. In other words, He can be grieved by anything in the life of an individual that is contrary to meekness, longsuffering, forbearing one another in love, and endeavoring to keep the unity of the Spirit in the bond of peace."[7]

It is vital to understand what grieves (saddens) the Spirit and causes Him to draw back from manifesting His presence in our lives. Carefully read Ephesians 4, which provides the context of what it means to grieve the Holy Spirit. (Pay close attention to verses 1-6 and 17-32).

What *attitudes, mindsets,* and *behavior* mentioned in verses 17-24 grieve the Holy Spirit?

_____

_____

_____

_____

_____

Ephesians 4:17-24 exposes *lifestyle choices* and *thinking* that sadden the Spirit and separate us from His manifest presence.

Sum up the *overall activity* in verses 25-31 that saddens the Spirit. Take time to also write the specific actions revealed in the passage.

Ephesians 4:25-31 reveals the specific *ways we treat others* that bring sorrow to the Spirit and separate us from Him.

Yes, we can sadden the Spirit, but the good news is we can also *gladden* Him! Carefully read verses 1-7, 14-15, 25, 29, and 32 and name the kinds of conduct that make the Spirit happy.

Consider the antonyms (opposites) of what grieves Him when developing your answer.

The key to *not* grieve the Holy Spirit is to pursue and preserve a spirit of *purity* and *oneness*. While pride and impurity paralyze the work of the Spirit, *humility* unleashes it. *Get quiet before God.* Ask Him, "Am I doing anything to grieve You?" Repent of anything He reveals, and ask for His grace to walk in humble, pure ways that gladden Him and invite His activity in your life.

YOU ARE THE HOLY SPIRIT'S HOME

Surely you know that you are God's temple and that God's Spirit lives in you!

—1 Corinthians 3:16 GNT

God Almighty—the all-knowing, all-powerful Creator of everything from microscopic molecules to gargantuan galaxies—has chosen to make His home in *your* heart! Yes, as a believer, the very same Spirit that raised Jesus Christ from the dead lives in you!

Pastor, author, and Greek scholar **Rick Renner** shares what it means to be home to God's Spirit:

> "When the Holy Spirit came into your heart, He made a home that was so comfortable, He was actually happy to come live inside you! He moved in, settled down, and permanently took up residency in your heart—*His new home!*
>
> You see, when you got saved, the ultimate miracle was performed inside your heart. The Holy Spirit took your spirit, which had been dead in trespasses and sin, and raised it to new life. His work inside you was so glorious that when it was all finished, He declared you to be His own workmanship (Ephesians 2:10). At that moment, your spirit became a *marvelous temple of God!*"[8]

Every place you go, every conversation you have, and every activity you participate in, you take God's Spirit with you. Stop and think about that.

How does this truth *encourage, excite,* and *strengthen* you? How does it shape your prayers?

Consider God's promises in Ephesians 3:14-20; Luke 12:11-12; John 14:12-17; Colossians 1:27; 2 Timothy 1:13-14 and Romans 8:1-17.

How does this truth *challenge* and *convict* you? How do your answers move you to pray?

_____

_____

_____

_____

Consider your choices in the entertainment you watch and listen to, the people you hang out with, and the activities you participate in.

So how would you describe your current level of communion with the Holy Spirit? Are you enjoying fellowship, partnership, and intimacy? Are you hearing His voice and experiencing His real, manifest presence in your life? Is it time for a good "spring cleaning" so He can feel more comfortable and at home in you? Pray and ask Him to reveal the condition of your heart. What is He saying? What steps is He asking you to take?

_____

_____

_____

_____

And so, dear brothers and sisters, I plead with you to give your bodies to God because of all he has done for you. Let them be a living and holy sacrifice—the kind he will find acceptable. This is truly the way to worship him.
Don't copy the behavior and customs of this world, but let God transform you into a new person by changing the way you think....

—Romans 12:1-2 NLT

DISCUSSION QUESTIONS

If you are using this book as part of the Messenger Series on the Holy Spirit, please refer to video session 2.

We have **communion** with the Holy Spirit.

> Communion is the Greek word *koinonia*, which means "fellowship, companionship, communication, intimacy, sharing together, social intercourse, partnership, joint participation, close mutual association." These types of communion can be broken down into three basic categories: fellowship, partnership, and intimacy.

1 | The Holy Spirit wants to have unbroken communion (*koinonia*) with us as sons and daughters of God. This communion includes *fellowship*, a friendly relationship of sharing life together. Why is it important to welcome and be keenly aware of the Holy Spirit's companionship? What might happen if we don't?

2 | In addition to fellowship, the Holy Spirit wants to be in *partnership* with us. What are some practical things partners do to help one another achieve success? What is unique about our partnership with God's Spirit today in comparison to that experienced by Old Testament followers of God, like Abraham or Moses? How does this encourage you?

3 | Communion with the Holy Spirit goes even deeper than just fellowship and partnership. It also includes *intimacy*—close, mutual association. How can we as believers develop this level of communion with the Holy Spirit?

> ### HONOR
> Any expression of respect or of high estimation by words or actions.
> In essence, to honor is to value, esteem, respect,
> treat favorably, and have high regard for.
>
> —adapted from *American Dictionary of the English Language*, **Noah Webster 1828**

4 | The Holy Spirit's primary function is to reveal who Jesus is and to bring Him honor and glory. He will reveal Christ and manifest Himself where He is genuinely honored. Carefully read the definition of *honor*. What are some specific ways we can honor the Holy Spirit individually and corporately as His Church?

5 | Although the Holy Spirit (Spirit of God) is never described as a female in Scripture, His behavioral patterns are at times feminine by function. Carefully read Genesis 1:27 and explain what this says about God's character, which includes the character of the Holy Spirit. How does knowing this truth affect your relationship with Him?

6 | The Holy Spirit is very gentle, tender, and comforting in nature. If we are not careful, we can *grieve* or *quench* the Spirit—we can sadden Him greatly and cause Him to draw back His activity in our lives. Carefully meditate on Ephesians 4:29-32 and identify some of the actions that grieve the Spirit. How is this *grieving* different from *quenching* the Spirit, as talked about in 1 Thessalonians 5:19-22? How can we guard against these actions?

7 | Every sin known to man is forgivable by God except one: *blaspheming the Holy Spirit*. Read Jesus' warning in Matthew 12:22-32 (also in Mark 3:22-30 and Luke 12:10). In light of these verses, describe what it means to blaspheme the Holy Spirit. Why do you think Jesus spoke so strongly against this?

NOTES

CHAPTER SUMMARY:

- The Holy Spirit desires ongoing *communion* with us.

- Communion includes fellowship, partnership, and intimacy.

- *Fellowship* is staying connected through communication and sharing life together.

- *Partnership* is about working together; it adds action to our communication.

- *Intimacy* is the deepest level of friendship in which we share our most personal thoughts, desires, and secrets with the Holy Spirit and He shares His with us.

- The Holy Spirit, who is fully God, has chosen to make His home in our hearts (spirits) permanently.

- We must be careful not to grieve Him, for He is tender and gentle and can be greatly saddened by our actions.

3

Three Levels of Relationships

"For the sake of your tradition *(the rules handed down by your forefathers), you have set aside the Word of God [depriving it of force and authority and making it of no effect]. You pretenders (hypocrites)! Admirably and truly did Isaiah prophesy of you when he said: These people draw near Me with their mouths and honor Me with their lips, but their hearts hold off and are far away from Me. Uselessly do they worship Me, for they teach as doctrines the commands of men."*

—Jesus (Matthew 15:6-9 AMP)

Day 1

Jesus made this sobering statement to the Pharisees because they had allowed a *tradition* to take precedence over the Word of God. My dictionary defines *tradition* as "an inherited, established, or customary pattern of thought, action, or behavior." Obviously, tradition, in and of itself, is not necessarily a bad thing. There are many great traditions that I celebrate with my friends and family. However, the Pharisees had elevated tradition (a customary pattern of thought) over God's Word, which made the Word of no effect in their lives. This truth is just as valid today. We must ensure that our understanding of truth is defined by the Word of God, not by the transient feelings, traditions, or philosophies of men.

Jesus went on to explain that the Pharisees' tradition created a breach in their relationships with the Creator. In fact, He declared that it was useless for them to even worship God because they had more faith in the doctrines (teachings and understanding) of men. True intimacy with

God would never have been an option for the Pharisees unless they repented of their blindness and embraced the truth. Likewise, in order for us to enjoy an intimate relationship with the Spirit, we must put aside the thoughts and traditions of men and embrace the truth about Him that is clearly evident in His Word. Otherwise, like the Pharisees, our attempts at an intimate relationship with God will be of no effect.

The Ultimate Teacher

Before I became close with the Spirit, I would read my Bible and think, *I love God with all my heart, but this is a bit dry.* The truth was, I was not asking the Holy Spirit to be part of my time of prayer and study. What I have discovered is that only the Holy Spirit makes the Scriptures come alive in my heart. Through His guidance, the Bible becomes much more than mere words—it becomes the very substance of life. In 2 Corinthians 3:6 we read:

> He has enabled us to be ministers of his new covenant. This
> is a covenant not of written laws, but of the Spirit. The old
> written covenant ends in death; but under the *new covenant*,
> the Spirit gives life. (NLT)

Our "new covenant"—expressed through the Word of God—is not just a list of rules and regulations. Rather it is life itself, and in turn breathes life into those who are subject to its rule. We can only enjoy the fullness of this new covenant through the Spirit, because He is the One who reveals the awesome mystery of who we are in Christ (which is the message of the New Testament). This is why we must invite the ultimate Teacher, the Spirit, into our times of study.

Have you ever had a teacher who wasn't passionate about what he or she was teaching? I have found those to be the worst classes. Getting through the syllabus is like suffering a root canal. Likewise, have you ever had a teacher who simply dislikes his or her students? What a miserable experience. The great news is that the Holy Spirit is passionate about revealing the mysteries of God's Word, and He is also extremely passionate about you! His desire is to see you walk in every gift that Christ made freely available to you. If we ask and seek, He will faithfully reveal the mysteries of life to us.

Atmosphere and Presence

Unfortunately, it seems that we often try to walk out this amazing Christian life without the presence and council of our Guide. In fact, the Holy Spirit is practically a stranger in many of our churches today. We have unknowingly substituted a good atmosphere for His presence. It is almost as if we have discouraged the manifestation of God's Spirit because a few individuals have responded to or attempted to manufacture His presence in a "weird" way.

Don't get me wrong; I believe we need great atmospheres in our church services. There have been many necessary cultural changes in the Church over the last several years, and one of these has been an upgrade in atmosphere. In many ways, the Church has become more relevant and attractive to the world. I believe this pleases God. As Paul stated, "I, too, try to please everyone in everything I do. I don't just do what is best for me; I do what is best for others so that many may be saved" (1 Corinthians 10:33 NLT). We have done a great job capitalizing on individual creativity and the advancement of technology; some of the most innovative places I have been to are churches. The Body of

Christ should be the innovators, the ones who are consistently driving creativity to new levels. But the Church will never fully step into her position of power, love, and authority on this earth if she does not invite the Holy Spirit into all her affairs. Remember, He is the senior partner in the relationship.

The good news is that we can have both a great atmosphere *and* His manifest presence. I am so thrilled when I get the opportunity to visit churches that excel in both of these areas. Don't allow yourself to fall prey to the notion that the manifestation of the Holy Spirit's presence will deter people from entering the kingdom. We must remember that the lost were drawn to, not repelled by, the apostles because of their partnership with the Holy Spirit. Any progress we as the Church achieve outside of the Spirit's involvement will waste away into nothingness.

Even Jesus, the Son of God, did nothing until He had received the power of the Holy Spirit (see Luke 4:1-15). We read in Luke 4:14-15, "Then Jesus returned *in the power of the Spirit* to Galilee, and news of Him went out through all the surrounding region. And He taught in their synagogues, being glorified by all." Notice this scripture states that He "returned in the power of the Spirit." This passage is an account of what took place after the forty days Jesus spent in the wilderness, where He was tempted by the devil. After leaving the desert *in the power of the Spirit*, Jesus returned to Nazareth and declared:

> *The Spirit of the Lord is upon Me*, because He has anointed Me
> to preach the gospel to the poor; He has sent Me to heal the
> brokenhearted, to proclaim liberty to the captives and recovery
> of sight to the blind, to set at liberty those who are oppressed;
> to proclaim the acceptable year of the Lord. (Luke 4:18-19)

It was because Jesus operated in the power of God's Spirit that He was able to accomplish His Father's will on the earth. Likewise the Church, by this same power, is to preach the gospel to the poor in spirit, bring healing to the brokenhearted, proclaim liberty to the captives, usher in clarity of sight, liberate the oppressed, and demonstrate the truth that God's hand is not too short to save. But we will never advance this heavenly cause if we do not *rely on the power of the Spirit.* Jesus needed the Spirit's power—what makes us any different?

Day 2

"More of Jesus"

My burning desire is for those who frequent our churches to experience the manifest presence of Jesus Christ. I hear people say all the time, "We need more of Jesus in our churches," and I completely agree with this sentiment. But who reveals Jesus to us? The Holy Spirit. As we learned earlier in this study, the Holy Spirit is not a commodity to be desired; rather He is a Person to be honored and invited. Why wouldn't we want the Spirit of truth present in everything we do? As Jesus once told His disciples:

> I still have many things to say to you, but you cannot bear
> them now. However, when He, the *Spirit of truth,* has come,
> *He will guide you into all truth;* for He will not speak on His
> own authority, but whatever He hears He will speak; and He
> will tell you things to come. He [The Holy Spirit] will glorify
> Me [Jesus], for He will take of what is Mine and declare it to
> you. All things that the Father has are Mine. Therefore I said
> that He will take of Mine and declare it to you. (John 16:12-15)

The Holy Spirit glorifies Jesus. It is through the Holy Spirit that Jesus is revealed to us. We cannot circumvent what God has established. If we want more of Jesus in our lives, we must walk in closer communion with the Holy Spirit. This is why the Holy Spirit is called the Spirit of Christ (see 1 Peter 1:11; Romans 8:9). When the Spirit speaks to us, He is representing Jesus. The Holy Spirit is not merely a "nice addition" to this life in Christ but rather the essence of Christ on the earth. The manifestation of His presence will not be found where He is not honored. Therefore, if we refuse to honor the Spirit, Christ's presence and power will be absent from our lives. Could this be why the world (the target of Christ's transforming power) often perceives the Church as both lifeless and powerless?

Deep Friendship with God

The end goal of communion is deep, personal friendship. The Spirit of God desires to be your friend. In fact, He yearns for your close fellowship. James said, "The Spirit who dwells in us yearns jealously" (James 4:5). What does He yearn for? He yearns for intimacy with you and me. Isn't that what we all desire to have with those we are closest to? Notice that He yearns *jealously*. This simply means He is not going to tolerate our entertainment of other suitors, even as my wife would never share the intimate secrets of her heart with me if I were courting another woman.

God desires our full devotion. Just one verse earlier in James, we read, "Friendship with the world is enmity with God" (James 4:4). The dictionary defines *enmity* as "a feeling or condition of hostility; hatred; ill will; animosity." These are strong words. It stands to be asked, why does friendship with the world create enmity with God?

Friendship with the world is the lust of the flesh. It is the selfish pursuit of gain, status, or position. It is the indulgence of our carnal selves. The Holy Spirit knows that our pursuit of these aims will only lead to futility and emptiness. God, in His jealous love, hates when we flirt with things that will only lead to the demise of our souls. Never forget that God is the perfect Father; like any great father, He hates to see His children settle for anything less than the best. This is why He will not tolerate our friendship with the world. Jesus desires for you to experience abundant life (see John 10:10), and the Holy Spirit manifests the desires of the Son. Remember that the Godhead is one in purpose. God passionately longs for an intimate relationship with His children. When we flirt with the world, we displace ourselves from the experience of deep intimacy with God. What a tragic loss—and how it breaks our Father's heart!

Far Beyond Salvation

I have come to realize that God's intentions for us go far beyond salvation. It is not "good enough" for us to stop at "being saved." Yes, the reality of our salvation is so wonderful that it is beyond our comprehension; but a place in heaven is only the beginning of all God wants to give us. God also sent His Son so that we can enjoy an amazing life on this earth. Why? Because it is really difficult for us to effectively advance His kingdom when we are constrained by the fears and desires of this world.

Paul once said, "Godliness is profitable for all things, *having promise of the life that now is* and of that which is to come" (1 Timothy 4:8). Notice the word *godliness*. Only someone who knows God can possess godliness *because godliness is to be like God*. I find it difficult to be like someone I am rarely around. When we spend time with people, they typically start to rub off on us. This is why James follows his statement about friendship with the world with, "Draw near to God and He will draw near to you" (James 4:8). God wants to spend time with you so that you can become like Him. We become godly through intimate knowledge of God, and the only way we can develop this deep relationship with God is through His Spirit (see 1 Corinthians 2).

Often when believers read, "Friendship with the world is enmity with God," they immediately try to completely distance themselves from the world. This, of course, makes no sense. How can the Church ever win the world if it detaches itself from humanity? As a Church, we must look to Jesus as our model. The lost were drawn to Jesus. He spent time with tax collectors and prostitutes, the very people the religious leaders looked down upon. He even attended their parties—but something was different about Him. Jesus was the ultimate example of what it means to be in the world but not of it. His heart broke for those the religious zealots shunned. Why was He so committed to the people the "godly" despised? Because He knew they were humble and hungry for a greater purpose. He did not attend their parties to be a part of what they pursued; He was there to show them a new way.

Likewise, we are called to reach out to the morally depraved and broken. If the Church will not be Christ's hands and feet, then who will? We—and we alone—are His Body. Through the transformational power of grace, we are now *in* Christ. We serve as His ambassadors (an extension and representation of who He is) on the earth. If we do not carry God's truth and light to this world, no one will.

Day 3

The Silent Gentleman

As I have walked with the Holy Spirit, I have discovered that He is a gentleman. He will never impose His will on us. If we refuse to engage with Him, He will be silent.

I have been traveling and ministering for over twenty-five years. During this time, I have noticed something about the drivers who pick me up from airports. They are always kind and extremely helpful, providing pertinent details and instructions for my stay and time of ministry. But typically, they will not speak to me unless I engage them in conversation. This is because their pastors instruct them not to, in case I need to work or prepare for the service while in the car. I have had many wonderful, servant-hearted drivers over the years and am very grateful for them. For this reason, I make a point of asking my driver about his family and his connection to the church. If I don't initiate, we may go the whole car ride without any meaningful conversation.

I believe we find a similar attribute in the Holy Spirit. He will not engage us unless we first position ourselves to hear His voice. If we do not engage with Him, He often remains quiet. Remember, James said God draws near to us when we draw near to Him. We are responsible for taking the first step. We have to intentionally enter into this awesome communion with Him. Put simply, the greatest invitation of all time has been extended to you. Now it is up to you to take action.

This truth is unknown to many believers. For this reason I often hear comments like, "Why isn't God talking to me?" or, "God hasn't spoken to me in years." Well, are these individuals pursuing communion with God as the Bible outlines we should? If we want to be close to God, we must seek to know Him—and this means we pursue friendship with the Person of His Spirit.

I encourage you to actively pursue communion with the Holy Spirit. You will be amazed by how He responds. Like many of my drivers, He will remain in your company whether you interact with Him or not because He has promised to never leave or forsake you (see Hebrews 13:5). But if you don't engage Him, He will generally remain silent, and you will never enjoy the full expression of His presence in your life or the benefits of communion with Him.

The Deep Things of God

Let's take another look at John 16:

> There is so much more I want to tell you, but you can't bear it now. When the Spirit of truth comes, he will guide you into all truth. He will not speak on his own but will tell you what he has heard. He will tell you about the future. He will bring me glory by telling you whatever he receives from me. All that belongs to the Father is mine; this is why I said, "The Spirit will tell you whatever he receives from me." (John 16:12-15 NLT)

This statement came during some of Jesus' final moments with His disciples before His crucifixion; a little later that evening Jesus was arrested by Roman officers and led away to be condemned to death. Clearly this was a moment deserving of weighty words.

Notice that Jesus says, "There is so much more I want to tell you, but you can't bear it now" (verse 12). Jesus was everything to these men. They had been with Him for years. Each one had left family, friends, and vocation to follow Him. The disciples were probably thinking, *What in the world do we need to do to get the full picture?* But then Jesus made an extraordinary promise: "When the Spirit of truth comes, he will guide you into *all truth*" (verse 13). In other words, "Even though I am present with you now (in the flesh), you are not in a position to receive everything I have to give. But I am sending you the Holy Spirit, and He will speak My words, reveal My will, and prepare you for what is to come." What a promise! Recall Jesus' previous words from that same evening:

> Nevertheless I tell you the truth. It is to your advantage that I go away; for if I do not go away, the Helper will not come to you; but if I depart, I will send Him to you. (John 16:7)

Hopefully these words are beginning to take on a new light. God is not playing hard to get—quite the opposite. All of us desire to be intimately known by the ones we love. The same is true of God. When Jesus walked the earth, He was the exact representation of His Father made available and accessible to man (see Hebrews 1:1-3; Colossians 1:15-19). But as we know, Jesus now abides at the right hand of the Father in heaven. The Holy Spirit is the Person of the Godhead who dwells with and in God's people on the earth, so to know the deep things of God, we must know His Spirit—the Spirit of truth.

Doubting Thomas

After Jesus was raised from the dead, ten of the disciples were in a room with the doors locked. Suddenly Jesus appeared; the disciples were completely amazed and in shock. Jesus actually had to convince them that He was not a ghost. The ten rejoiced over the miracle of His resurrection, and they later shared this account with Thomas, who had not been present with them at the time of Jesus' appearing. Upon hearing the news, Thomas infamously replied, "Unless I see in His hands the print of the nails, and put my finger into the print of the nails, and put my hand into His side, I will not believe" (John 20:25).

Several days later, all eleven disciples were together in a room when Jesus suddenly appeared again. Before doing or saying anything else, He immediately turned to Thomas, as if to say, "Okay, Thomas, let's take care of this matter of unbelief." He told him, "Reach your finger here, and look at My hands; and reach your hand here, and put it into My side. Do not be unbelieving, but believing" (John 20:27). Thomas responded, "My Lord and my God!" Now listen to what Jesus proceeded to say:

> Thomas, because you have seen Me, you have believed. *Blessed are those who have not seen and yet have believed.* (John 20:29)

In essence Jesus was stating, "Thomas, there is a blessed group of people who will believe without seeing." I used to think, *Jesus that is kind of hard. I mean, the guy is already groveling on the floor. He obviously feels terrible. He's repentant! And yet You looked at him and said, "Blessed are those who have not seen and yet have believed."* I couldn't understand why Jesus was so hard on Thomas. Then one day the Lord spoke to me, "I wasn't rebuking Thomas; I was simply making a statement of fact. The level of intimacy available to those who know Me by My Spirit is much greater than that of knowing Me in the physical sense."

Day 4

Three Levels of Relationships

So what exactly did Jesus mean when He made this statement to Thomas? To answer, allow me to explain why a deeper intimacy can be achieved by faith than by sight.

There are three levels of relationship: the physical level, the soul level, and the spiritual level. The lowest (most superficial) level is the *natural* or *physical* level. Many romantic relationships begin here, with thoughts like: *She's good-looking*, or *He's good-looking, so maybe we should get together.* Unfortunately, a lot of couples only have a relationship on this level when they get married. They think, *I can ignore the fact that we don't get along very well or that we really don't talk and connect on issues or common interests, because I'm attracted to him or her.* In these cases, the soul level is underdeveloped. The wedding bells chime, the honeymoon ends, and then life happens. This couple will have to realize that they need to establish a deeper level of intimacy with each other or they will suffer a miserable marriage. If they don't commit to a deeper connection, the woman will pursue her interests with her friends, and the man will pursue his interests with his friends. They will wind up merely coexisting. This was never God's intention for marriage.

The next level of relationship is that of the *soul* or the *personality* of a person. This is the level of relationship that existed between David and Jonathan: "...the soul of Jonathan was knit to the soul of David, and Jonathan loved him as his own soul" (1 Samuel 18:1). When Jonathan was killed, David lamented, "I am distressed for you, my brother Jonathan; you have been very pleasant to me; your love to me was wonderful, surpassing the love of women" (2 Samuel 1:26). David was not talking about a perverted physical relationship. There was no physical attraction between them. Their connection was that of the soul and completely free of any unnatural physical aspect. Yet they were able to build a bond much deeper than that of a merely physical relationship (which is what David meant when he said "the love of women").

The soul level is the level on which marriages should be built. Don't get me wrong, the physical aspect of a relationship is very important. I am extremely attracted to my wife; she is the most beautiful woman in the world to me. But there are much deeper levels of relationship that can and should be achieved between husbands and wives. The fact is, Lisa's personality is more endearing to me than her physical beauty.

Sadly, I have heard numerous stories about men and women leaving their spouses for someone they met online. A few years ago I was preaching at a church where a gentleman walked up to me after the service. He was surrounded by six young children. Two were in his arms, two were holding onto his legs, and two were running around in the foyer. Because the man had such a depressed look on his face, I asked him, "Sir, are you okay?" He said, "Not really. Today my wife left me and our six children for a man she met on the Internet." Her "soul" relationship with this other man had developed to the point that she was willing to leave her husband after many years of marriage. The soul tie was even strong enough to separate this mother from her natural inclination to care for and be with her children.

The soul level of relationship often requires little or no physical interaction. This is why relationships that start off as long-distance relationships often end up being some of the best marriages. Without the potential distractions of physical attraction, the couple is able to focus on the development of their soul connection.

The Highest Level of Relationship

The highest or deepest level of relationship is the *spiritual* level. This is the level Jesus was referring to in His conversation with Thomas. Paul once said, "For who among men knows the thoughts of a man except the spirit of the man which is in him?" (1 Corinthians 2:11 NASB). In other words, you cannot know the true thoughts or motives of a man unless you are in tune with his spirit.

As I previously mentioned, Lisa and I recently celebrated our thirtieth anniversary. Some of my favorite memories from that time together are of us sitting by the pool and discussing the things of God. We even spent a lot of time talking about this message. As I shared what God was putting in my heart, she responded with wisdom and revelation that further illuminated what the Spirit had been revealing to me. Since we both have an intimate relationship with the Spirit, we are able to commune on a deep, spiritual level.

This is also one of the main reasons why Lisa and I pray together. It connects us spiritually because we are fellowshipping *together* around the things of the Spirit. For a similar reason, we have mandated that the staff of Messenger International spend the first fifteen minutes of every day in corporate prayer. We do this because we want our team to be spiritually connected. It is amazing what this time of prayer has done for the relationships between our staff members. The same is true in any relationship: fellowship around the Word and prayer will develop the deepest level of intimacy between individuals because it is a spiritual connection.

There is a difference between an intellectual discussion of spiritual things and true spiritual fellowship. Sometimes people start talking to me about the Bible, and I know they are merely relaying information. How do I know this? What they are saying is very tiring, and my mind becomes exhausted. They are speaking from their minds, not their spirits. Then there are others who speak of spiritual things from their spirits. I have talked with these people for hours without tiring because we are connecting on a spiritual level.

Knowing God by His Spirit

Now let's look at 1 Corinthians 2:11 in its entirety:

> For who among men knows the *thoughts* of a man except the
> spirit of the man which is in him? Even so the *thoughts* of God
> no one knows except the Spirit of God. (NASB)

The Greek word here translated as *thoughts* is best defined as "state of being or the composition of." Paul is essentially saying that one cannot know the true "composition" of God (meaning the deep matters of His heart) without coming to know the Spirit of God. By "know," I mean have an understanding that is much more than the superficial knowledge that can be obtained with little or no effort. Practically everyone in the United States knows who our president is, but most of us do not have a personal relationship with him. We do not know his deepest desires, what drives him, or what he truly believes. Likewise, we will never possess anything more than "common knowledge" about God if we do not discover Him by His Spirit.

Paul continues, "Now we have received not the spirit of the world, but the Spirit who is from God, that we might understand the things freely given us by God" (1 Corinthians 2:12 ESV). What an amazing statement. No one knows the thoughts of God except His Spirit (verse 11), but He has given us that Spirit! Through relationship with the Spirit of God, we can now have intimacy with the Creator *on the spiritual level – the highest level of relationship.*

Paul went to this level with the Spirit. Although he never physically walked with Jesus, he said, "But I make known to you, brethren, that the gospel which was preached by me is not according to man. For I neither received it from man, nor was I taught it, but it came through the *revelation of Jesus Christ*" (Galatians 1:11-12). How was Jesus revealed to Paul? Paul clearly states that this revelation did not come from any man. If he didn't receive this revelation from man, and he didn't spend time with Jesus in the flesh, then he must have received this revelation through *the Spirit of Christ* (the Holy Spirit).

Is it possible that Paul was actually able to go to a greater depth in his relationship with Jesus because he never physically walked with the Savior? Peter, one who had physically interacted with Jesus, wrote a letter toward the end of his life in which he stated, "...our beloved brother Paul also wrote to you with the wisdom God gave him—speaking of these things in all of his letters. *Some of his comments are hard to understand...*" (2 Peter 3:15-16 NLT). Peter was the one who had conversed with Jesus face to face every day for years. He was present when Jesus was glorified on the Mount of Transfiguration. He witnessed the crucifixion and then saw and fellowshipped with Jesus after the resurrection. Yet this disciple—one who had enjoyed years of interaction with Jesus in the flesh—said that some of Paul's revelations from the Spirit were hard to understand. I personally believe this shows that Paul entered a greater depth in his relationship with Jesus than Peter did.

By the Spirit's inspiration, Paul wrote the majority of the books in the New Testament, yet he never walked with Jesus. How could he do this? Because the Spirit is the One who fully reveals Jesus. Remember Jesus' words: "There is so much more I want to tell you, but you can't bear it now. When the Spirit of truth comes, he will guide you into all truth [give you the full revelation]" (John 16:12-13 NLT). Paul couldn't base his faith in Jesus on previous physical interactions with Him, because he never had any. He had to believe and receive apart from seeing. In essence this removed any aspect of the physical that could have fought against what the Spirit was attempting to show him. This is what Jesus was referring to in His interaction with Thomas. The fact that Paul did not have a physical relationship with Jesus to fall back on meant that he had to totally rely on his *spiritual* relationship with the Master. He had no other choice.

Like Paul, you and I have been given the opportunity to follow Jesus without any possible conflicts of previous misunderstandings developed through physical interaction. The awesome truth is that we can become closer to Jesus without seeing Him than we would have by seeing Him. Without the ability to physically walk with Jesus, we have to commune with Him through the Spirit of Christ who dwells within us—thus establishing a deep, spiritual relationship with God. How amazing!

Experience Him on the Deepest Level

God knows that our flesh is (for now) unredeemed. Our spirits are redeemed; they are in the exact likeness and image of Jesus (see 1 John 4:17). Our souls are in the process of being redeemed (see James 1:21). But our physical bodies have not yet experienced redemption.

Have you ever noticed how easily we grow tired of things? Some people can buy a new car and it becomes old news just one week later. This is the nature of unredeemed flesh. The physical has very little depth; it is short-lived and will soon pass away. So God in His goodness says, "I'm not revealing Myself to My people physically. I'm going to make a way for them to commune with Me by My Spirit so they can really know Me." It's almost like God is saying, "I'm going to have a long distance relationship with the ones I love so they can really get to know My heart."

As a church, we are the Bride of Christ. God is preparing us for a vibrant marriage with Him. He is allowing us to get to know Him on the deepest level (spiritual) before we ever know Him on a physical level. This is why Paul later wrote, "From now on, we regard no one according to the flesh. Even though we have known Christ according to the flesh, yet now we know Him thus no longer" (2 Corinthians 5:16). We know Him by the Spirit—the Spirit of the living God. There was a time when Christ was revealed in the flesh. But now, since He is no longer physically on the earth, we have the opportunity to know Him by the Spirit.

If we neglect to enter into communion with the Spirit, we deny ourselves the opportunity to know the Son. The Spirit searches all things within the heart and mind of God to reveal Jesus to us. If you want a deep relationship with God, you must move beyond superficial knowledge of Him and enter into the journey of discovering who He truly is. This journey is only possible through communion with the Spirit. This is why we cannot hold any traditions (customary patterns of thought) related to the Holy Spirit that are not rooted in the eternal Word of God. When we allow misconceptions, personal bias, or negative experiences to skew our understanding of the Spirit, we will not enjoy the full promise of God's glorious presence in our lives. We cannot know God apart from His Spirit.

I believe you can have a relationship with the Spirit where you desire what He desires and feel what He feels. The deepest level of relationship—the spiritual level—is available to you. On this level, you will discover an intimacy with your Creator unlike any other. But you must seek to know who the Holy Spirit is if you are to walk in close communion with Him. How can you know Him? By reading His Word and spending time in His presence. God wants to draw near to you; all you have to do is take the first step in drawing near to Him.

Take a moment to meditate on the verses below and allow the Spirit to do a work in your heart. As you turn to God, ask Him to remove any mind-set (veil) that has kept you from the experience of His presence. Once these veils are removed, you will be able to behold Him like never before. As you look upon His face (spend quality face time with Him as His intimate friend), He will transform you into His likeness. I leave you with these words from the apostle Paul:

> But whenever someone turns to the Lord, the veil is taken away.
> For the Lord is the Spirit, and wherever the Spirit of the Lord
> is, there is freedom. So all of us who have had that veil removed
> can see and reflect the glory of the Lord. And the Lord—who
> is the Spirit—makes us more and more like him as we are
> changed into his glorious image. (2 Corinthians 3:16-18 NLT)

WELCOME HIM AS YOUR TEACHER

You have received the Holy Spirit, and he lives within you, so you don't need anyone to teach you what is true. For the Spirit teaches you everything you need to know, and what he teaches is true—it is not a lie. So just as he has taught you, remain in fellowship with Christ.

—1 John 2:27 NLT

The Holy Spirit plays many roles in our lives, but probably His greatest role is that of Teacher. He is always teaching us something. He is the perfect parent who permanently lives within, bringing direction and correction in His tender, loving way.

Scripture is the timeless textbook of the Spirit. God's Word is the record of God's thoughts. To think like Him, talk like Him, and act like Him, we need His Word—and we need to understand it. That's the job of our Teacher: to lead us and guide us into all truth, unfolding the meaning of the scriptures we need, right when we need them. Author and pastor **Francis Frangipane** eloquently states:

> "The Word of the Lord, united with the Holy Spirit, is the vehicle of our transformation into the image of Christ. ...The Word is God. The Scriptures are not God but the Spirit that breathes through the words is God. And this Holy Spirit should be honored as God. Therefore, as you seek the Lord...pray that you will not merely read intellectually. Rather, ask the Holy Spirit to speak to your heart through the Word. ...As you kneel in humility before the Lord, the Word will be engrafted into your soul, actually becoming a part of your nature (James 1:21)."[1]

Stop and ask yourself, *How do I approach God's Word? Do I invite my Teacher to teach me? Do I read into it or receive from it?* Now, ask the Spirit, "What can I do differently to see the Word come alive and become a part of my nature?" Write what He reveals and put it into practice.

_____

_____

_____

Is devotional time the only time the Spirit teaches? No. He is teaching *all the time*, and if you're in tune with Him, there is a lesson to learn at every turn. Frangipane suggests:

> "...Carry a pad and pen with you at all times. ...We are called to *abide* in Him, not just visit with Him. ...You must develop such a listening ear that the Spirit could speak to you anywhere about anything. Honor Him and He will honor you."[2]

This could look differently for every person. Use whatever medium or technology works best for you. The important point is that you listen and remember what He speaks.

Carefully meditate on these verses. What is the Spirit revealing about the Word in your life?

2 Timothy 3:16-17; 2 Peter 1:12-21

_____

_____

Deuteronomy 6:6; 11:18; Psalm 119:9-11; Colossians 3:16

_____

_____

Psalm 19:8; 119:105, 130; Proverbs 4:20-23; 6:20-23

_____

_____

Hebrews 4:12; James 1:21; Jeremiah 23:28-29

_____

_____

"Call to me and I will answer you. I'll tell you marvelous and wondrous things that you could never figure out on your own."

—Jeremiah 33:3 The Message

PLEDGE YOUR ALLEGIANCE TO HIM AS LORD

Jesus replied, "The most important commandment is this: ...The Lord our God is the one and only Lord. And you must love the Lord your God with all your heart, all your soul, all your mind, and all your strength."

—Mark 12:29-30 NLT

The Lord, who is the Spirit, loves us passionately and wants our love exclusively. He does not want our affection and attention attached to the world or anything in it. He says:

Don't love the world's ways. Don't love the world's goods. Love of the world squeezes out love for the Father. Practically everything that goes on in the world—wanting your own way, wanting everything for yourself, wanting to appear important—has nothing to do with the Father. It just isolates you from him. The world and all its wanting, wanting, wanting is on the way out—but whoever does what God wants is set for eternity.

—1 John 2:15-17 The Message

Check out these related scriptures: Matthew 16:24-26; Titus 2:12-14; James 4:4-6; John 15:18-21; Romans 12:2.

WHERE DOES YOUR ALLEGIANCE LIE? Take an honest inventory. Ask yourself:

Who or what gets the majority of my time and attention? What do I spend my free time doing?

_____

_____

Who or what excites me? Are technology and fashion trends in their proper places in my life?

_____

_____

99

What kinds of things do I spend my money on?

_____

_____

What's on my mind most? What do I frequently talk about? What subjects permeate my prayers?

_____

_____

Our words reveal our allegiances. Jesus said that what our hearts are full of is what spills out of our mouths (see Luke 6:45).

Review your answers. Ask the Holy Spirit, "Do I need You to adjust my priorities? Has something become an idol in my life? Is there anything that I'm chasing more than You?" What is He saying? What steps is He prompting you to take to redirect your allegiance to Him?

_____

_____

_____

_____

Meditate on God's words in Matthew 6:19-21 and Colossians 3:1-17. Use them to *write a prayer of dedication* asking the Holy Spirit to keep you loyal to the Lord your God.

_____

_____

_____

GROW GRADUALLY BY HIS GRACE

We are transfigured much like the Messiah, our lives gradually becoming brighter and more beautiful as God enters our lives and we become like him.

—2 Corinthians 3:18 The Message

Just before He went to the cross, Jesus made a key statement about the Holy Spirit: "I still have many things to tell you, *but you can't handle them now.* But when the Friend comes, the Spirit of the Truth, he will take you by the hand and guide you into all the truth..." (John 16:12-13 The Message).

As the All-knowing One, Jesus could have shared many truths with His disciples, but He knew they couldn't understand them yet. They needed time to grow. Once He died, rose again, and ascended into heaven, the Father sent His Spirit to help us grow gradually by His grace.

Would a good parent expect their newborn to understand multiplication? Or their toddler to know how to prepare taxes? No. Similarly, the Holy Spirit waits until we are mature enough to handle the truth He needs to tell us. He not only leads us into all truth about Scripture, He also leads us into truth about ourselves, our children, our health, our circumstances, and more.

According to God's Word, we grow (become like Jesus) from one level of faith and glory to another.[3] We have a part in this process, and so does the Holy Spirit. Carefully meditate on Philippians 1:6; 2:12-13; 1 Thessalonians 5:23-24 and Hebrews 13:20-21. What is the Spirit revealing to you in these verses about growing in Christ? Do you see a repeated theme?

_____

_____

_____

_____

_____

_____

England's best-known preacher during the latter nineteenth century, **Charles H. Spurgeon**, wrote prolifically on many topics, including the Holy Spirit and growing up spiritually. He said:

> "We trust in Jesus for what we cannot do ourselves. If it were in our own power, why would we need to look to Him? It is ours to *believe*; it is the Lord's [the Holy Spirit] to create us anew. He will not believe for us; neither are we to do regenerating work for Him. It is enough for us to *obey* the gracious command. It is for the Lord to work the new birth in us."[4]

Don't give into thinking, *I should be more spiritually mature.* It's not true. It only makes you feel condemned and drains you of spiritual strength. Pause and pray, "Holy Spirit, how do You see where I am right now (my level of spiritual maturity)?" What is He saying to you?

_____

_____

_____

The way the Spirit sees you is the way you should see yourself. Ask Him to give you grace to embrace the place you are so you can keep growing.

Have you been frantically trying to change yourself? If so, how? What do you see differently now?

_____

_____

_____

_____

VALUE THE DIVINE CONNECTIONS HE CREATES

Love from the center of who you are; don't fake it. ...Be good friends
who love deeply; practice playing second fiddle.

—Romans 12:9-10 The Message

We were made for relationship—relationship with the Father and with others. Think about it. What would your life be like without relationships? If you took away all of the life-giving connections, what would you have? A lonely, empty life.

Thank God for relationships! The value of a godly friend is priceless. A good friend sharpens us mentally, emotionally, and spiritually, like iron sharpens iron. A good friend lovingly exposes error and brings correction when needed. A good friend celebrates your successes and encourages you to press on through life's difficulties.

You are better off to have a friend than to be all alone, because then you will get
more enjoyment out of what you earn. If you fall, your friend can help you up.
But if you fall without having a friend nearby, you are really in trouble.

—Ecclesiastes 4:9-10 CEV

We have learned that there are three levels of relationships—physical, soul, and spiritual. How does seeing this help you understand your current relationships? With whom does it help most? Why?

_____

_____

_____

_____

_____

_____

The deepest, most meaningful connections we can have are on the spiritual level. Describe what this kind of relationship looks like. What are some benefits of fellowshipping on the spiritual level instead of just the physical or soul levels?

_____

_____

_____

_____

_____

Are there people with whom you would like to develop deeper relationships? Stop and pray, "Holy Spirit, what can I do to help cultivate deeper, spiritual relationships with the people you've put in my life?" Be still and listen. Write what He is speaking to you.

_____

_____

_____

_____

_____

Prayer for Divine Connections:
Holy Spirit, grant me divine connections. As Jonathan was to David, as Ruth was to Naomi, as John was to Jesus, so connect me with the people You want me in relationship with. Give me Your grace to cultivate healthy friendships, including those on a spiritual level. In Jesus' name, Amen!

For Further Study...
Proverbs 13:20; 17:9, 17; 27:6, 10, 17; John 15:13; 1 John 1:7; 1 Samuel 18:1-4

EXPERIENCE GOD ON THE DEEPEST LEVEL

...Learn to know the God of your ancestors intimately. Worship and serve him with your whole heart and a willing mind.

—1 Chronicles 28:9 NLT

God's greatest pursuit is to know us intimately, and He invites us to do life with Him. Could there be a greater quest? Paul said, "Everything else is worthless when compared with the infinite value of knowing Christ Jesus my Lord. For his sake I have discarded everything else, counting it all as garbage, so that I could gain Christ" (Philippians 3:8 NLT).

Experiencing the Depths of Jesus Christ was **Jeanne Guyon's** passion. So vital was this mission that she wrote a book by the same name. This seventeenth-century Frenchwoman influenced believers like John Wesley, Hudson Taylor, and Watchman Nee. Regarding intimacy, she said:

> "Let me ask you...do you desire to know the Lord in a deep way? God *has* made such an experience, such a walk, possible for you. He has made it possible through the grace He has given to *all* His redeemed children. He has done it by means of His Holy Spirit. How then will you come to the Lord to know Him in such a deep way? Prayer is the key."[5]

So, how would you describe prayer in relation to knowing God intimately? Carefully read Jesus' prayer in Matthew 6:5-15. What can you learn from Him and apply in your life?

_____

_____

_____

_____

_____

As we have learned, when we're born again, the Holy Spirit comes to live in our spirits. So, when the Spirit communicates with us, He does so in our *spirits*. Jeanne Guyon continues,

> "The Lord is found only within your spirit, in the recesses of your being, in the Holy of Holies; this is where He dwells. The Lord once promised to come and make His home within you. (John 14:23) He promised to there meet those who worship Him and who do His will. The Lord *will* meet you in your spirit ...Once your heart has been turned inwardly to the Lord, you will have an impression of His presence."[6]

The most intimate way we can know God is *by His Spirit*—His Holy Spirit whom He has given us (see 1 Corinthians 2:9-12). Stop and pray, "Holy Spirit, are there any misconceptions, bad experiences, or personal biases I have concerning You that are distorting my understanding of You?" Be still and listen. Ask Him to remove any mindset that's keeping you from His presence. Write what He reveals.

_____

_____

_____

Meditate on this truth and ask the Holy Spirit to reveal its meaning to your heart.

> *But whenever someone turns to the Lord, the veil is taken away. For the Lord is the Spirit, and wherever the Spirit of the Lord is, there is freedom. So all of us who have had that veil removed can see and reflect the glory of the Lord. And the Lord—who is the Spirit—makes us more and more like him as we are changed into his glorious image.*
>
> —2 Corinthians 3:16-18 NLT

DISCUSSION QUESTIONS

If you are using this book as part of the Messenger Series on the Holy Spirit, please refer to video session 3.

1 | Jesus said the Pharisees had allowed the *traditions of men* to trump the authority of God's Word. What are traditions of men, and why are they damaging to our communion with our Creator? Give at least one modern-day example of the traditions of men trumping the truth of God's Word.

2 | The Holy Spirit *yearns* to be our best friend and is jealous for our intimate fellowship. What things in the world would you say have stolen the attention and affection of the Church (believers) away from the Spirit? What will happen if we flirt with the world, seeking its pleasures, possessions, and status more than communion with the Spirit?

3 | What is Jesus communicating to the apostle Thomas in John 20:29? How is this truth connected with God's words through the apostle Paul in 2 Corinthians 5:16, and how does this truth make our intimate relationship with the Lord better?

4 | Name and describe the *three levels of relationships* that we can have with others. Which is the deepest level and why? How can we get connected with people on this level?

5 | We have been given a tremendous gift in the Holy Spirit: the ability to know God intimately. Carefully read 1 Corinthians 2:11-16. What is the Holy Spirit speaking in this passage about truly knowing God?

6 | Peter and the other disciples had an experience like no other—they
       interacted with Jesus face to face. Paul did not share this experience,
       yet he was still mightily used by God. How was this possible?

For more: Look up John 20:29; 2 Corinthians 5:16 and 2 Peter 3:15-16.

7 | What will happen to our relationships with God if we neglect to pursue
       communion with the Holy Spirit? If you are willing, share with your
       group some practical ways you have been able to connect with the
       Holy Spirit and experience His amazing friendship.

NOTES

CHAPTER SUMMARY:

- If we want a deep, intimate relationship with God, we have to know Him by His Spirit.

- Only the Spirit knows and reveals the thoughts, feelings, and purposes of God's heart.

- We have been given God's Spirit; He is the ultimate Teacher who guides us into all truth.

- To maintain friendship with the world—the selfish pursuit of status and pleasures—is to be God's enemy.

- The Holy Spirit is a gentleman; He will not force His will or friendship on us.

- The three levels of relationship are: physical (lowest and most superficial), soul (or personality), and spiritual (deepest and most intimate).

- Knowing God by His Spirit is deeper and more intimate than knowing Him only through interaction with the physical Person of Jesus.

4

Empowered by the Spirit

Take a moment to imagine a king from the Middle Ages. Try to envision his environment: the castle and turrets, knights and ladies-in-waiting, the battles, the kingdom, and his glory. The office and lineage of a king was often considered ordained by God, so kings were greatly revered by their subjects and lived in abundant wealth. The king's word was law and his judgments were final. A good king understood that his responsibility was to protect those who lived within his kingdom's boundaries; he was also in charge of pursuing the interests of the kingdom by extending its borders and securing additional resources.

There was a tremendous amount of responsibility placed on this position and, consequently, the king was granted extraordinary power—at times even absolute power. Keep in mind that I am not describing a figurehead (typical of our era, when democracies and republics serve as the most common forms of government). I am describing an absolute monarchy. Now imagine this sort of king rejecting or being completely unaware of the power that comes with his position. What would happen to his kingdom? Soon it would be conquered, its inhabitants enslaved, and its resources confiscated. It isn't enough for the king to simply hold the position of "king" (meaning he merely enjoys residence in the palace and the accompanying opulent lifestyle). He must perform the *functions of kingship* that are only made possible by the *power of his position*. The king's position of authority is of no effect if he does not wield the power that comes with it.

As children of God, we have become co-heirs with Christ. In Romans we read, "And since we are his children, we are his heirs. In fact, together *with Christ* we are heirs of God's glory" (Romans 8:17 NLT). This position is again made clear in Ephesians 2:6: "[God] raised us up together, and made us sit together in the heavenly places *in Christ Jesus*." In and through Christ, we have been repositioned. No longer are we children of this world, but rather we are royalty (heirs) in the kingdom of Heaven. As heirs in this kingdom, we have been charged with the advancement of our Lord's mission. His conquest and His kingdom have become our own because we have been adopted into His lineage. What a mind-blowing truth! But like the earthly king in our illustration, if we are to be effective in our position in Christ, we must discover and wield the power that comes with it. In this chapter we will delve into how we are empowered to fulfill our role in the advancement of His kingdom. Peter declared:

You are royal priests, a holy nation, God's very own possession.
As a result, you can show others the goodness of God, for he
called you out of the darkness into his wonderful light.
(1 Peter 2:9 NLT)

Before we continue further, it is important to note: position always precedes power. We must be positioned in Christ before we can ever do anything for His kingdom.

The Power We Need

And being assembled together with them, He *commanded* them
not to depart from Jerusalem, but to wait for the Promise of the
Father, "which," He said, "you have heard from Me; for John
truly baptized with water, but you shall be baptized with the
Holy Spirit not many days from now." (Acts 1:4-5)

Jesus did not *suggest* that the apostles should wait for the Promise, nor did He *recommend* that they heed His instruction. Rather, He "*commanded* them not to depart from Jerusalem" until the Promise had come. Jesus was compelled to place such high importance on this instruction because the empowerment of the Spirit is essential to all kingdom work. He knew His disciples were eager to share the good news of His resurrection and might grow restless in waiting for the promise of the Holy Spirit. In Acts 1:3 we learn that they had spent days with Jesus, hearing Him teach on the kingdom of God. The Bible states that the apostles had received "infallible proof" of His resurrection. They did not need to be persuaded of the validity of their cause because they had firsthand evidence of Christ's victory over death. In other words, they were ready to get going!

But Jesus looked at them and said, "Don't start your ministry. Don't start preaching the gospel all over the world, and don't start any churches until you have been clothed with the Spirit's power" (Luke 24:49, author's paraphrase). I believe Scripture shows Jesus gave this directive to approximately 500 people (see 1 Corinthians 15:6). But in Acts 1:15, we find that the number of people in the upper room had dwindled to 120. What happened to the other 380 people? I personally believe that with each day that passed, more and more of the original 500 left until only 120 remained. Maybe the 380 who left thought, *Let's go back to the synagogues, start churches, and share the wonderful news of Jesus' resurrection. After all, it wouldn't be right to waste a single day in sharing this good news.* Only 120 were willing to wait as the Master commanded.

At this point, you may be thinking, *Well, John, of course the disciples needed to wait for the Holy Spirit. They hadn't received Him yet. It's different for us now because we receive the Holy Spirit at salvation.*

Take a look at John 20:21-22:

"Peace to you! As the Father has sent Me [Jesus], I also send you." And when He had said this, He breathed on them, and said to them, "Receive the Holy Spirit."

Jesus breathed on the disciples and said, "Receive the Holy Spirit." The Greek word for *receive* means "immediately or right now."[1] This was not a foreshadowing of what was going to happen. The disciples actually *received* the Holy Spirit before Jesus ascended into heaven. But they were not clothed with power until they had been *filled* with the Spirit on the Day of Pentecost.

The Day of Pentecost

When the Day of Pentecost had fully come, they were all with one accord in one place. And suddenly there came a sound from heaven, as of a rushing mighty wind, and it filled the

whole house where they were sitting. Then there appeared
to them divided tongues, as of fire, and *one* sat upon each of
them. And they were all *filled* with the Holy Spirit and began
to speak with other tongues, as the Spirit gave them utterance.
(Acts 2:1-4)

I know that many of us have witnessed the flannelgraph version of this account in our Sunday school classes. Typically, the assembled believers are depicted as having little tongues of fire on top of their heads. This is probably not the best representation of what happened. In the Old Testament fire often symbolizes the presence of God. What the author of Acts described as "tongues, *as of fire*" is the manifestation of God's presence. These followers of Jesus, both men and women, were engulfed or baptized in God's presence. This revealed presence is also seen in the reference to a "rushing mighty wind." As we established in chapter one, the Holy Spirit is not a "mighty wind." He is a Person. However, the manifestation of His arrival in the upper room took the form of a mighty wind.

The Greek word for "filled" in Acts 2:4 literally means *satiated.*[2] According to the dictionary, *satiate* means "to supply to excess." Those in the upper room were filled *to excess* with the Holy Spirit. All of them experienced a greater degree of God's manifest presence in their lives. In addition to the manifestations of fire and wind, another sign of the infilling of the Spirit was the fact that the believers began to speak in other tongues.

Why Tongues?

A tongue is simply a language. If I were in Spain and met someone who clearly wasn't speaking Spanish, I could ask either, "What is your mother tongue?" or, "What is your native language?" They mean the same thing. In contrast I wouldn't need to ask someone who spoke English what his native tongue is because, as a native English speaker, I recognize the language. Therefore, to me English is a "known" tongue, whereas I might consider another language an "unknown" tongue. More on this later.

On the Day of Pentecost, Jews from many nations had gathered in Jerusalem for a religious celebration. As residents of various countries and regions, these Jews had many "mother tongues."

> And there were dwelling in Jerusalem Jews, devout men, from every nation under heaven. And when this sound occurred, the multitude came together, and were confused, because everyone heard them speak in his own language. Then they were all amazed and marveled, saying to one another, "Look, are not all these who speak Galileans? And how is it that we hear, each in our own language [tongue] in which we were born?" (Acts 2:5-8)

Notice the Bible states that "when this sound occurred, the multitude came together." These utterances drew many to those who were speaking in tongues. The multitude was astonished that the Galileans (many of whom were considered untrained or unlearned) were speaking in many different languages. This expression of God's Spirit was a sign to those who were not yet followers of Jesus.

"We hear them speaking in our own tongues the wonderful works of God." So they were all amazed and perplexed, saying to one another, "Whatever could this mean?" (Acts 2:11-12)

This outpouring of the Spirit created the opportunity for Peter to respond with one of the most famous sermons in the Bible, in which he said, "This Jesus God has raised up, of which we are all witnesses. Therefore being exalted to the right hand of God, and having received from the Father the promise of the Holy Spirit, He poured out this which you now see and hear" (Acts 2:32-33). Notice that everyone both *saw* and *heard* evidence of the Holy Spirit's power.

A few verses later, the crowd responded:

Now when they heard this, they were cut to the heart, and said to Peter and the rest of the apostles, "Men and brethren, what shall we do?" (Acts 2:37)

Peter told them:

"Repent, and let every one of you be baptized in the name of Jesus Christ for the remission of sins; and you *shall receive* the gift of the Holy Spirit. For the promise [the Holy Spirit] is to you and to your children, and to all who are afar off, as many as the Lord our God will call." (Acts 2:38-39)

As Peter declared the good news of salvation that has been made available to all who call on the name of the Lord (see Romans 10:13), he also made it abundantly clear that the gift of the Holy Spirit is available to everyone who believes. How amazing! This promise is available to every believer—past, present, and future.

Four Accounts

In the book of Acts, there are four additional accounts of people being filled with the Holy Spirit after the Day of Pentecost. As we go through these four accounts, I would like for you to pay special attention to two things. First, in all but one of the accounts, the infilling of the Holy Spirit is a separate occurrence from the salvation experience. Second, those who witnessed these infillings of the Spirit both *saw* and *heard* evidence of the Spirit's presence in the new believers.

Philip and the Samaritans

We find the first of these four accounts in Acts 8. Philip had been sent to the city of Samaria to share the gospel of Jesus Christ. As the gospel was declared, the whole city experienced revival. The lame were healed, unclean spirits were driven out, and many received the great news of God's salvation.

> But when they believed Philip as he proclaimed the good news
> of the kingdom of God and the name of Jesus Christ, they were
> baptized, both men and women. Simon himself believed and
> was baptized. And he followed Philip everywhere, astonished
> by the great signs and miracles he saw. (Acts 8:12-13 NIV)

When the Samaritans believed the good news of Jesus Christ, were they born again? Absolutely. When a person believes the gospel, he or she receives Jesus Christ and becomes a child of God. These new believers were then baptized in water as a sign of their faith in Christ. Yet as we see in the verses that follow, the leaders of the early Church knew there was something else—in addition to conversion and water baptism, the new believers needed to receive the baptism of the Holy Spirit.

> When the apostles in Jerusalem heard that Samaria had ac-
> cepted the word of God [*salvation*], they sent Peter and John to
> Samaria. When they arrived, they prayed for the new believers
> there *that they might receive the Holy Spirit*, because the Holy
> Spirit had not yet come on any of them; they had simply
> been baptized in the name of the Lord Jesus [*water baptism*].
> (Acts 8:14-16 NIV)

Upon hearing that Samaria had received the gospel, the apostles
decided to send Peter and John to the new believers there. Why did the
apostles send two of their most respected members to pray with the Samaritans? After all, the Samaritans had already received salvation and
been water baptized. Peter and John were sent specifically to pray "that
they might receive the Holy Spirit" (verse 15). Keep in mind that Jerusalem was over thirty-five miles away from Samaria.[3] This distance may
not seem like much today, but the apostles did not have cars or access to
modern public transportation. They had to travel these thirty-five miles
by foot or on the back of an animal, a journey that would have taken at
least one or two days. This was no quick trip down the street.

Again, it is important to note that the new believers had been
baptized in the name of the Lord Jesus. They were now children of
God. However, there was an element of the gift of salvation that they
had not yet experienced. You might be thinking, *Wait a second, John, I
thought that the Spirit of Jesus Christ makes our hearts His home as soon as
we receive the gift of salvation.* Indeed, this is the case. First Corinthians
12:3 clearly states, "No one can say that Jesus is Lord except by the
Holy Spirit." We cannot confess the lordship of Jesus outside of the Holy
Spirit's influence, yet this is different from being *filled* with Him.

The Bible makes it clear that all who are in Christ are sanctified and sealed by the Holy Spirit (see 1 Peter 1:2; Ephesians 1:13). So there is no doubt that receiving the indwelling *presence* of the Holy Spirit is part of the salvation experience. When God sees you, He sees the Spirit of His Son. Remember, when you receive salvation, you are repositioned in Christ—you become part of His heritage and His kingdom. However, you are not filled with the Spirit's *power* until you ask it of the Father. Jesus said:

> If you then, being evil, know how to give good gifts to your
> children, how much more will your heavenly Father give the
> Holy Spirit to those *who ask Him*! (Luke 11:13)

Jesus called God "*your* heavenly Father"; therefore, it is evident that He is speaking of believers. We know this because in John, Jesus refers to "the Spirit of truth, *whom the world cannot receive*, because it neither sees him nor knows him" (John 14:17 ESV). The "world" represents those who exist outside of God's kingdom. Clearly, anyone who has not submitted to Jesus' lordship cannot receive the Holy Spirit. So this instruction to ask "your Father" for the Spirit is not a reference to salvation. It pertains instead to a later infilling that can only be received by those who are already saved.

Now, let's return to Acts 8:

> Then Peter and John laid their hands upon these believers, and
> they received the Holy Spirit. When Simon *saw* that the Spirit
> was given when the apostles laid their hands on people, he of-
> fered them money to buy this power. "Let me have this power,
> too," he exclaimed, "so that when I lay my hands on people,
> they will receive the Holy Spirit!" (Acts 8:17-19 NLT)

Peter and John laid their hands upon the believers, and they received the Holy Spirit. This infilling of the Spirit was clearly evident to the physical senses because the Bible says that "Simon *saw* that the Spirit was given when the apostles laid their hands on people." Simon, who was a believer, was so amazed by the manifestation of the Holy Spirit's *power* in the believers that he offered to pay the apostles to teach him how to impart this power. (This response was inappropriate, and Peter was quick to rebuke Simon.)

Throughout Acts, the infilling of the Spirit was typically followed by an outward manifestation that could be *seen* and *heard*—most commonly in the form of tongues and prophecy. This is why the apostles would often say that the Holy Spirit would "come upon" believers. This account in Samaria is one of the few instances where the Bible does not specifically say that tongues and prophecy followed the infilling of the Spirit. However, we can deduce that such a demonstration did occur; otherwise Simon, a former sorcerer, would not have seen the evidence of the Spirit's presence in the believers.

Day 3

Saul of Tarsus

The story of Saul's conversion is one of the most notable passages in Scripture. I want to focus on what is perhaps a less prominent aspect of this amazing encounter. In Acts 9, we find Saul on his way to persecute the believers in Damascus:

As he journeyed he came near Damascus, and suddenly a light shone around him from heaven. Then he fell to the ground, and heard a voice saying to him, "Saul, Saul, why are you persecuting Me?" And he said, "Who are You, Lord?" Then the Lord said, "I am Jesus, whom you are persecuting...." So he, trembling and astonished, said, "Lord, what do You want me to do?" Then the Lord said to him, "Arise and go into the city, and you will be told what you must do." (Acts 9:3-6)

Notice that Saul called Jesus "Lord." When Jesus Christ becomes Lord of our lives, we are immediately born again. I believe Saul became a believer the moment he recognized Jesus' lordship.

After this encounter with the Lord, Saul spent the next three days fasting in the city and awaiting further instruction. Then the Lord asked a disciple named Ananias to go to Saul. Ananias was concerned about this directive because he had heard many stories of how vigilantly Saul persecuted believers. So God told him, "Go, for he [Saul] is a chosen vessel of Mine to bear My name" (Acts 9:15). Upon arriving at the house where Saul was staying, Ananias placed his hands on Saul and said, "*Brother Saul*, the Lord Jesus, who appeared to you on the road as you came, has sent me that you may receive your sight and *be filled with the Holy Spirit*" (Acts 9:17). Ananias obviously knew that Saul had received salvation, for he called him "Brother Saul." Yet even though Saul was a believer, Ananias was still sent by God to specifically pray that Saul would receive healing and the infilling of the Holy Spirit.

Again, in this instance, we see that the infilling of the Holy Spirit occurred after the gift of salvation had already been received. In Acts 9, you will not find any mention of Saul (also called Paul) speaking in tongues. However, we do know that Paul spoke in tongues because he later wrote, "I thank God that I speak in tongues more than all of you" (1 Corinthians 14:18 ESV). Personally, I believe Paul began speaking in tongues when Ananias prayed for him. Paul had to receive this infilling even though he was already saved, because the empowerment of the

Holy Spirit was vital in Paul's efforts to declare Jesus before Gentiles, kings, and the children of Israel (see Acts 9:15).

Peter and Cornelius

In Acts 10 we get a little glimpse into our God's sense of humor. Verse one introduces us to Cornelius, a Roman officer. The Bible says that Cornelius was a devout and God-fearing man who was gracious to the poor and frequently prayed to God. At this point, the gospel of salvation had not been communicated to the Gentiles, so God sent an angel to visit Cornelius. However, the angel did not reveal God's plan for salvation to Cornelius; rather, he told Cornelius to send for Peter. In his excitement, Cornelius immediately sent men to find Peter at the place where the angel had indicated.

We next learn that Peter was residing in Joppa when he fell into a trance and received a vision from heaven. In this vision, God used various forms of imagery to communicate to Peter that he should not call unclean what God had made clean (see Acts 10:9-15). Obviously, God knew that Peter would have a hard time understanding the meaning of what he had seen because He gave Peter the same vision three times. As Peter pondered its meaning, Cornelius' men arrived at the house. The Holy Spirit instructed Peter to go with them. God did not tell Peter why he was being sent to see Cornelius, even though it was against the custom of the day for devout Jews to associate with Gentiles. Upon arriving at Cornelius' house, Peter said:

> You know it is against our laws for a Jewish man to enter a
> Gentile home like this or to associate with you. But God has
> shown me that I should no longer think of anyone as impure or

unclean. So I came without objection as soon as I was sent for. Now tell me why you sent for me. (Acts 10:28-29 NLT)

Peter was starting to draw the connection between the vision and his encounter with this devout Gentile, so he began to preach the gospel to Cornelius. Suddenly, in the middle of Peter's message, the Spirit of God manifested, and the Gentiles began speaking in tongues. Peter was completely shocked because this had never happened before.

God knew that Peter and his Jewish traveling companions would have a hard time coming to terms with the fact that the gift of salvation was also intended for the Gentiles. So God poured His Spirit out on the Gentiles *before* Peter ever had a chance to pray with them or baptize them in water. This was proof that those outside the nation of Israel were also included in the plan of salvation.

The Jewish believers who came with Peter were amazed that the gift of the Holy Spirit had been poured out on the Gentiles, too. For they *heard* them speaking in other tongues and praising God. Then Peter asked, "Can anyone object to their being baptized, now that they have received the Holy Spirit just as we did?" So he gave orders for them to be baptized in the name of Jesus Christ. (Acts 10:45-48 NLT)

The Jews could not deny the evidence of God's salvation among the Gentiles because they *saw* and *heard* the manifestation of God's power among them (the infilling of the Holy Spirit). The Jewish believers were shocked. Not only had God made salvation available to the Gentiles, but He had also sent the infilling of the Spirit before the normal order of public confession and water baptism had been fulfilled. This is the only instance in Scripture where you will find God operating in this manner.

In every other instance the outpouring of God's Spirit occurs *after* conversion. I believe God did this because He knew the Jews required a special sign that He was extending His gift of salvation to the Gentiles as well.

The Ephesians

The fourth account that I want to examine is found in Acts 19. Paul was in the midst of one of his many journeys when he came to Ephesus. Upon his arrival, the Bible says that he encountered some disciples of John the Baptist. The very first question he asked them was, "Did you receive the Holy Spirit when you believed?" (Acts 19:2). Wow! If this was the first thing Paul asked these Ephesians, it should be one of the first questions we ask any new believer.

Again, why was this issue so important to the early Church leaders? Because the empowerment of the Holy Spirit is essential to our mission in Christ. Why would any of us ever want to live an hour without the power to fuel that mission (see Acts 1:8)? To be effective in the Father's kingdom, we must be both positioned in Christ (salvation) and empowered by the Holy Spirit (infilling of the Spirit).

Paul discovered that though these Ephesians were disciples of John the Baptist, they had not heard the good news of salvation through Jesus, so he began to share the gospel with them.

As I mentioned before, receiving our position in Christ will always precede the empowerment of His Spirit. Even if, as in the case of Cornelius, the outward manifestation of power (the infilling of the Spirit) precedes the outward confession of salvation (in the form of water baptism), salvation always comes before empowerment.

Therefore, after hearing Paul's words, the Ephesians were first "baptized in the name of the Lord Jesus" (Acts 19:5). In other words, they received the salvation that is only in and through Jesus Christ. But the encounter did not end there: "And when Paul had laid hands on them, the Holy Spirit came upon them, and they spoke with tongues and prophesied" (Acts 19:6).

The infilling of the Holy Spirit occurred after the new believers had been baptized in the name of our Lord Jesus. Before their encounter with Paul, these men knew very little about Jesus. But once they were filled with the Spirit, they *prophesied*, which means they declared the message of Jesus Christ. This empowerment to prophesy what they had not known just minutes earlier was made possible only by the Spirit. It is impossible for a believer to declare with authority the mysteries of God without first knowing His Spirit (see 1 Corinthians 2).

I am so thankful that I never have to preach without the empowerment of the Spirit. In my own strength, I am not a good public speaker. Likewise, I am not a good writer. I was so bad at English that I flunked my SAT. My exact score was 370 out of 800. No one knows better than I do that I am what I am by the grace of God and the empowerment of His Spirit. Without the Spirit's empowerment, I could not write this book. He is the source of my ability and strength. Without Him my kingdom assignment would be impossible. The Holy Spirit is the "Manifester" of God's grace to me.

Day 4

Have Tongues Ceased?

Love never ends. As for prophecies, they will pass away; as for tongues, they will cease; as for knowledge, it will pass away. For we know in part and we prophesy in part, but when the perfect comes, the partial will pass away. (1 Corinthians 13:8-10 ESV)

Now that we have examined accounts of the infilling of the Holy Spirit from the book of Acts, I want to address a question many of you may have. I often hear people say that tongues have ceased. These people are generally referencing the statement made in this passage from 1 Corinthians 13. Individuals who subscribe to this idea believe that Paul was referring to the Bible as "the perfect" when he said, "When the perfect comes, the partial will pass away." The line of reasoning is, *Now that the perfect (the Bible) has come, tongues have ceased.*

It is important that we carefully examine this passage to determine what Paul was saying. When we consider the context of this verse, it is clear that this notion is impossible. If tongues have ceased, then knowledge and prophecy have also ceased. Have knowledge and prophecy ceased? Certainly not. So what is "the perfect" that Paul is referring to? The answer is found in verse twelve:

> For now we see in a mirror dimly, but then [when the perfect comes] face to face. Now I know in part; then I shall know fully, even as I have been fully known. (1 Corinthians 13:12 ESV)

Paul is describing face-to-face encounter with Jesus. This is what he means by "the perfect"—knowing Jesus fully in His glory. Are we currently experiencing this kind of encounter with Jesus? Are we beholding Him in His glory? During our lives on earth, our experiences with Jesus are like the reflection in a dim mirror. But in the age to come, we will know Jesus *as He knows us.* This experience of deepest intimacy with Jesus is the sign that "the perfect" has come. Though this journey begins on earth, it will not be completed until we behold Him face to face in eternity.

The Four Types of Tongues

Another question I am frequently asked is, "John, why does 1 Corinthians 12:30 say, 'Do all speak with tongues?' Doesn't this mean that not everyone speaks in tongues?" Yes, it does. However, in this passage Paul is referring to a specific *type* of tongue; not all believers operate in this *type* of tongue. To understand this, we must examine the four different types of tongues discussed in the New Testament.

For the sake of our discussion, I will refer to these tongues as being for *public* or *private* use. Two types are for public ministry. By "public" I mean that they involve one individual ministering something of the Spirit to another person or group of people. In contrast, the two "private" tongues connect us as individuals directly to God—either by increasing our intimacy with Him or by enabling us to intercede according to His perfect understanding. Let's take a look at each of these.

One: Tongues As a Sign to Unbelievers

The first type of tongues is for public demonstration.

> Therefore tongues are for a sign, not to those who believe but to unbelievers. (1 Corinthians 14:22)

These tongues occur when the Holy Spirit transcends our intellect and gives us the ability to speak another language of this earth, specifically a language that we do not know how to speak from our own experience or education. This is the type of tongue that operated through the disciples on the Day of Pentecost.

Now there were staying in Jerusalem God-fearing Jews from every nation under heaven. When they heard this sound, a crowd came together in bewilderment, because each one heard their own language being spoken. Utterly amazed, they asked: "Aren't all these who are speaking Galileans? Then how is it that each of us hears them in our native language? Parthians, Medes and Elamites; residents of Mesopotamia, Judea and Cappadocia, Pontus and Asia, Phrygia and Pamphylia, Egypt and the parts of Libya near Cyrene; visitors from Rome (both Jews and converts to Judaism); Cretans and Arabs—we hear them declaring the wonders of God in our own tongues!" (Acts 2:5-11 NIV)

These Jews heard the believers speaking in each of their native earthly tongues. This demonstration was a sign that God was at work among those who believed the gospel of Jesus, because there was no way the untrained Galileans could perfectly declare the wonders of God in so many languages. Many came to know Jesus because of this expression of the Spirit's power.

Several years ago I was preaching at a church in Colorado Springs. During the service one of my staff members was sitting in the back of the church. The whole time I was preaching, she felt the urge to quietly pray in tongues. When the service was over, a gentleman who was sitting in front of her approached her and said, "Your French is perfect. You even speak with a perfect accent of the ancient French dialect. I'm a French teacher, and in all my years, I've never encountered someone who speaks French as well as you do."

My staff member responded, "I don't speak French." The man was shocked!

He said, "Not only were you speaking perfect French, but you were also quoting scriptures in French. Then John would have the congregation turn to those same scriptures. You quoted them before he even said them." This experience was a sign to the man affirming the message that God had released through me. The primary purpose of tongues as a sign is to grab the attention of one who is not yet a believer.

Two: Tongues for Interpretation

The second type of tongue is also for public ministry. Unlike tongues as a sign, these tongues are heavenly languages that are not spoken anywhere on the earth. *Tongues for interpretation* are the type of tongues Paul referred to as a spiritual gift when he said, "...to another *different kinds of tongues*, to another the *interpretation of tongues*" (1 Corinthians 12:10). Since these tongues are not languages of this earth they have to be interpreted.

Years ago I was getting ready to preach at a church in Singapore. All of a sudden, a man in the service began to speak in an unknown tongue. I knew right away that this tongue was not a language of the earth; it was a heavenly language. Everyone in the room was amazed by this manifestation of the Spirit. After he finished speaking in this heavenly tongue, the man then began to give the interpretation. His interpretation was exactly in line with the message that God had given me for the church. I thought, *God, thank You so much for this amazing confirmation!* God used this gifting of *tongues for interpretation* to affirm the word He had placed in my heart. It was a sign for me and for all those in attendance.

Notice that I use the word *interpret*, not *translate*, with this kind of tongue. Heavenly tongues (which account for three of the four types of New Testament tongues) cannot be translated, for they transcend our human understanding—but they can be interpreted.

Any expression of tongues that falls under *tongues for interpretation* should always come with an interpretation. Without this interpretation the Church cannot be edified, and this tongue is exclusively given for the Church's edification (see 1 Corinthians 14).

This is the type of tongue Paul was referring to when he asked, "Do all speak in tongues?" Now let's look at this verse in context:

God has appointed these in the church: first apostles, second prophets, third teachers, after that miracles, then gifts of healings, helps, administrations, varieties of tongues. Are all apostles? Are all prophets? Are all teachers? Are all workers of miracles? Do all have gifts of healings? Do all speak with tongues? Do all interpret? (1 Corinthians 12:28-30)

Paul is speaking of the public gifts which God has ordained for ministry in the Church. Are all apostles? No. Are all prophets? No. Are all teachers? No. Likewise, do all speak in or interpret tongues *as a public ministry*? No. Paul's point is that we should all flourish in the specific gifts that God has placed on our lives. Not everyone in the Church will operate in tongues as a public ministry.

The Difference Between the Two Public Tongues

Later in his letter to the Corinthians, Paul explains the difference between the two types of public tongues:

Therefore tongues [*tongues for a sign*] are for a sign, not to those who believe but to unbelievers…. Therefore if the whole church comes together in one place, and all speak with tongues [*tongues for interpretation*], and there come in those who are uninformed or unbelievers, will they not say that you are out of your mind? (1 Corinthians 14:22-23)

If you do not understand that there are different types of tongues, you might think that Paul completely contradicted himself when he wrote this. First he said, "Tongues are a sign for the unbeliever." Then, in the very next verse, we read, "If you speak with tongues, unbelievers will think you are out of your mind." However, with a better understanding of the four distinct tongues, we can see that Paul is writing about two different types of tongues.

The first type of tongue Paul mentions (tongues for a sign) is the type that draws unbelievers because it serves as a sign to them. The second type of tongue (tongues for interpretation) is only meant for the Church's edification; these tongues are not signs to the unbeliever. In fact, Paul states that without interpretation, the act of believers speaking in the second kind of tongues would actually cause unbelievers to think we are crazy!

Can you imagine a Sunday morning service where everyone was preaching, teaching, or prophesying at the same time? That would be bizarre and ineffective. Likewise, Paul was instructing the Church not to create an environment of confusion by misappropriating tongues for interpretation. In the wrong setting, this expression of tongues is chaotic and purposeless. Earlier in this same chapter Paul makes it clear that tongues are not to breed confusion, but rather to bring understanding and revelation.

I thank my God I speak with tongues more than you all; yet *in the church* I would rather speak five words with my understanding, that I may teach others also, than ten thousand words in a tongue. (1 Corinthians 14:18-19)

It is pretty simple: if a public tongue is used, it must be interpreted for the benefit of those present. Otherwise, it would be better to simply communicate in a known language.

Three: Tongues for Personal Prayer

For if I *pray in a tongue*, my spirit prays, but my understanding is unfruitful. What is the conclusion then? I will pray with the spirit, and I will also pray with the understanding. I will sing with the spirit, and I will also sing with the understanding.
(1 Corinthians 14:14-15)

The first two types of tongues we discussed are for public expression and communicate a message from God to men. Tongues for a sign are intended to reach out and minister to the unbeliever; tongues for interpretation are intended to minister to the believer. In the verses above, Paul introduces the third type of tongues: *tongues for personal prayer.* He is no longer talking about public ministry; rather he is teaching about tongues to be used for private purposes. This form of tongue is for personal edification and prayer. Paul specifically states that we can "pray with the understanding," which for me would mean praying in English, or we can "pray with the spirit," which means praying in an unknown language—a heavenly one. He also declares that we can sing (worship) either way as well.

Earlier in 1 Corinthians 14 we read, "He who speaks in a tongue does not speak to men but to God" (verse 2). We know this manifestation of the Spirit could not refer to tongues as a sign, because on the Day of Pentecost, the disciples were speaking to men—declaring the wonderful works of God in foreign languages. Paul also couldn't be speaking of tongues for interpretation, for this gift refers to a believer speaking to a church in an unknown heavenly language (which would need to be interpreted). Here Paul is specifically addressing a person who, in the spirit, "is not speaking to men but to God."

Speaking in tongues for personal prayer is a private interaction between God and the one praying. Its purpose is to strengthen the one who is praying. "But you, beloved, building yourselves up in your most holy faith and praying in the Holy Spirit, keep yourselves in the love of God" (Jude 20-21 ESV). Notice Jude states that when we pray in the Holy Spirit (in tongues) we build ourselves up; however, when we speak in tongues for interpretation to believers in the Church, we edify or build up the Church (see 1 Corinthians 14:5). God desires both, and each is important.

Many believers wonder, *Is it possible for me to be filled with the Holy Spirit and not pray in tongues?* Yes, I believe a person can be filled with the Spirit and not pray in tongues. But I would also add that every person who has been filled with the Spirit *has the ability* to pray in tongues. Many believers do not operate in this gift because they have not yet yielded to it by faith. Every gift of God is received and activated by faith.

Think of it this way. Two men walk out into a river. One chooses to stand still and allow the current to flow around him; the other chooses to relax and yield to the river's flow. Both the one who stands in the river and the one who yields to it are in the water, but only the latter is able to follow the current where it leads. The one who prays in tongues can be likened to one who yields to the river's current; a believer who has yet to pray in tongues is likewise in the river but has not yielded to its current. (If you want to know how to yield to the Spirit, we will discuss this in the next chapter.)

Communion with the Holy Spirit is one of the many blessings made available to us through Jesus' death and resurrection. But the experience of the full measure of this communion does not automatically occur at the moment of salvation. Sadly, many believers are not enjoying certain aspects of the gift of salvation. It is vital that we pursue *all* God has for us. Discovering all that Jesus died to give us is a huge part of our journey in Christ. As we discussed earlier, the Holy Spirit is the one who empowers and equips us for our kingdom assignments. If we forsake the gifts made available to us by the Spirit, we forgo both deeper intimacy with God and a measure of the power we need to serve Him well.

Four: Tongues for Intercession

Likewise the Spirit also helps in our weaknesses. For we do not know what we should pray for as we ought, but the *Spirit Himself makes intercession for us with groanings which cannot be uttered.* Now He who searches the hearts knows what the mind of the Spirit is, because He makes intercession for the saints according to the will of God. (Romans 8:26-27)

Paul begins this passage by saying that "the Spirit also helps in our *weaknesses.*" What weakness is Paul referring to? The answer: "For we do not know what we should pray…but the Spirit Himself makes intercession for us with groanings which cannot be uttered." Simply put, our weakness is that we have limited understanding of what is going on in our world. Therefore, there are times when we do not know how to pray. But when we rely on and intercede in the Spirit (who knows all things), He prays the perfect will of God through us.

When I was in college, I led a Bible study that reached out to fraternities and sororities on Purdue's campus. It was attended by about sixty students, some with no church background, and others from various church denominations. One girl who attended the study had been raised in a denomination that believed tongues have passed away. After hearing me teach on the Holy Spirit one night, she realized, *Tongues are for today! There it is in the Bible!* That same night she was filled with the Holy Spirit.

The next day, I was awakened by a call at 6:30 a.m.—far earlier than I, a college student, wanted to be awake! I was being summoned to meet the girl from the Bible study, whose sorority was across the street from my fraternity house. I dragged myself out of bed and walked outside to where she was waiting for me.

I was half asleep and a little irritated by the early morning interruption. She, on the other hand, was ecstatic. I said, "What's going on?"

She replied, "God woke me up at five o'clock. I felt this urge to pray in tongues, so I just started praying. It really felt like I was interceding. I asked God to show me why I was praying so fervently in tongues. The Lord said, 'You're praying and interceding for an older man's life.' So I just kept praying in tongues.

"Then at six o'clock, my roommate got an emergency call. She was told that her grandfather had experienced a heart attack and had been rushed to the hospital. They were able to save him."

She continued, "The Holy Spirit spoke to me and said, 'You were praying for him.'" This is a perfect example of tongues spoken for intercession. She had no idea that this man's life was in jeopardy, but the Holy Spirit knew. If she could only pray with her understanding she wouldn't have been able to intercede for him.

My mother lives in Florida, so I don't know exactly what is going on in her life right now. I don't know what is going on with my sister who lives in California. But the Holy Spirit knows the perfect will of God for both of them, and He will intercede through me as I yield to partner with Him in prayer. The Spirit searches all things and knows all things. Great peace accompanies the knowledge that we are allowing the Holy Spirit to pray through us!

Clarification About Private Tongues

It is important to note an exception regarding the two types of tongues I have referred to as "private." There are occasions when believers who are all filled with the Spirit pray together in tongues. In these times, it is appropriate for all of them to pray together in the Spirit. There are other times when believers should refrain from praying publicly in their prayer languages. Paul made this statement:

> Therefore if the whole church comes together in one place, and all speak with tongues, and there come in those who are *uninformed* or *unbelievers*, will they not say that you are out of your mind? (1 Corinthians 14:23)

Two groups are identified in this passage. First, Paul mentions *unbelievers*. This refers to those who have not received Jesus Christ as their Lord—those who are outside the faith. The second group is the *uninformed*. These people are believers in Jesus, but they have not been taught about the language of the Spirit. A person belonging to either group would be uncomfortable in an atmosphere where others pray together in tongues. They could easily think of those speaking, *Are you out of your mind?*

Sadly, I have witnessed one or two instances in Sunday morning worship services where many people were praying aloud in tongues all at once—and were encouraged to do so by leadership. In fact, in the past, I have even led people in this way because of a lack of understanding. In these services, as in a typical Sunday morning service, there were most likely visitors present, many of whom would fall into the categories of *unbelievers* or *uninformed*. They probably thought to themselves, *Are these people out of their minds?* I have observed that these churches struggle in growing and reaching their communities. Could the reason be that they are not following the wisdom given in 1 Corinthians 14:23? I believe if they continue this practice, the *uninformed* and *unbelievers* will not return.

On the other hand, there are times when a church calls for a believers' prayer meeting (say, on a Saturday morning or Monday evening). In these meetings all are *informed* and *believers*. It is perfectly fine for all to pray in tongues as a group when gathered in ministry to the Lord or for intercession.

Simply put, Paul is not saying that there is never an appropriate time or place for a group of believers to gather and speak together in what we might call "private tongues." He is simply making the distinction that in "public," when *unbelievers* or the *uninformed* are present in our midst, our expressions of tongues must be appropriate to our environment.

God's Desire for You

Therefore, brethren, desire earnestly to prophesy, and *do not forbid to speak with tongues*. Let all things be done decently and in order. (1 Corinthians 14:39-40)

Paul knew that the Church would mishandle the amazing gift of tongues. So he urged us, "Use the right type of tongue in the right setting, and do not forbid speaking in tongues because certain believers have misappropriated this extraordinary gift of the Spirit." Unfortunately, the Church is ignorant of many things of the Spirit. This is tragic, because the Holy Spirit is the One who has been sent to empower the Church. God has chosen His Church as the vehicle by which He advances His kingdom. If we do not wake up to the power that comes with our position in Christ, we will be no different than a king who refuses to wield the power of his throne.

How many believers are missing out on these amazing gifts of the Spirit because they believe that tongues have passed away? God's heart is clear: "I wish you all spoke with tongues" (1 Corinthians 14:5). Some may argue, "That's Paul writing, not God." All Scripture is authored by the inspiration of God, and this verse is no exception (see 2 Timothy 3:16).

Never forget that the gift of tongues is a vital aspect of the empowerment of the Holy Spirit—as well as a beautiful part of our intimate relationship with God. So my hope for you is the same as Paul's: I pray you embrace this remarkable gift and grow in the power and presence of the Spirit every single day.

THE SPIRIT BRINGS *ACTION!*

God confirmed the message by giving signs and wonders and various miracles and gifts of the Holy Spirit whenever he chose.

—Hebrews 2:4 NLT

The Holy Spirit is the Agent of action who manifests in many amazing ways. In Scripture, He is symbolically represented as a *dove, fire, wind,* and *wine.* Understanding these manifestations helps us understand His character and how He desires to work in and through our lives.

The Spirit is like a *dove.* In all four gospels, the Spirit is described as descending on Jesus like a dove. Doves are gentle and loving in nature; they are very timid and easily driven away. They will only come to rest where they feel safe and at peace. When they choose a mate, it's for life. How do these facts help you better understand and relate to the Holy Spirit?

_____

_____

_____

Check out Matthew 3:16-17; Mark 1:9-11; Luke 3:21-22; John 1:32-33

The Spirit is like *fire.* He manifested in a burning bush to Moses and a pillar of fire to Israel.[1] On the Day of Pentecost, the Spirit baptized people in "divided tongues, as of fire" (Acts 2:3). He is the Fire that Jesus brought to earth, and we must be careful not to quench Him. Think about the characteristics of fire: it purifies, gives light, produces warmth/heat, and consumes things. How does this help you understand the fire of God's Spirit in your life? What fuels the Fire and helps fan the flame?

_____

_____

_____

Check out Acts 2:3-4; Luke 12:49; 1 Thessalonians 5:19-21; Matthew 3:11-12; Luke 3:16-17; Jeremiah 20:9; 23:29; Hebrews 12:29

The Spirit is like *wind*. He manifested on the Day of Pentecost not only as fire, but also as wind. Winds can range from a gentle breeze to hurricane force. Think about what wind does. How might the wind of the Spirit bring action in the seasons of your life? What might He cause?

_____

_____

_____

_____

Check out John 3:5-8

The Spirit is like *wine*. At Pentecost, the disciples spoke in tongues declaring the wonders of God. The manifestation was so remarkable that some said they had drunk too much wine, but Peter said it was the Spirit! Stop and think. How does drinking wine usually affect a person's emotions? How might drinking the new wine of the Spirit affect you?

_____

_____

_____

Check out Acts 2:13-18; Luke 5:37-38 (also in Mark 2:22; Matthew 9:17); Ephesians 5:18-19; Esther 1:10; Jeremiah 31:11-13

"Heaven cannot contain the Holy Spirit, yet He finds a home within the hearts of His servants. We are His temple. Each one of His influences will evoke from us grateful praise. If He is like the wind, we will be like wind chimes; if He is like dew, we will bloom with flowers; if He is a flame, we will glow with ardor. In whatever way He moves within us, we will be responsive to His voice."

—Charles H. Spurgeon[2]

HIS PRESENCE PRODUCES *EVIDENCE*

The evidence of the Spirit's presence is given to each person for the common good of everyone.

—1 Corinthians 12:7 GW

When the Spirit of God is present, there is evidence! Rivers and seas give way to dry ground. Blind eyes and deaf ears are opened. The lame walk and the mute talk. Fear is defeated and hope is reborn! Signs and wonders of all kinds mark the landscapes of our lives as we are knitted in relationship with God's Spirit.

Again and again, the accounts in Acts confirm that when the Holy Spirit was present, people *saw* and *heard* the evidence. Look back over your life. What evidence of the Spirit's presence can you remember? Write a sentence or two describing situations in which the Spirit showed up and radically changed your life.

I remember when _____

_____

_____

I remember when _____

_____

_____

I remember when _____

_____

_____

Don't rush. Meditate on God's goodness. Let the Spirit reinvigorate you with new life as you recall His faithfulness!

*Once again I'll go over what God has done, lay out on the table the
ancient wonders; I'll ponder all the things you've accomplished,
and give a long, loving look at your acts.*

*O God! Your way is holy! No god is great like God! You're the God who
makes things happen; you showed everyone what you can do.*

—Psalm 77:11-14 The Message

The Holy Spirit has helped you before, and He desires to do it again! How
do you need Him to help you now? Get quiet before Him, and invite Him to
do it again! Ask Him to show evidence that He is real and really cares about
you and those around you. Be still. What is He speaking to you?

_____

_____

_____

_____

Pause and offer praise to the Lord. **Write a prayer** of praise and thanks to
Him. He is worthy!

_____

_____

_____

_____

BEING FILLED IS AN ONGOING *EXPERIENCE*

Don't be drunk with wine, because that will ruin your life.
Instead, be filled with the Holy Spirit.

—Ephesians 5:18 NLT

God's command through Paul to be *filled with the Holy Spirit* is vital. The Greek word for *filled* is *pleroo* ("play-ro-o"). It means "to fill and disperse throughout one's soul."[3] Even more important is the tense of this verb: passive, imperative, present. The **passive** voice implies that "you" (the subject) are *to be acted upon;* the **imperative** voice makes it *a command,* not a suggestion; and the **present** tense aspect implies *continuous action.*

Ephesians 5:18 in the *Amplified Bible* nails this truth: "And do not get drunk with wine, for that is debauchery; but **ever be filled** and stimulated with the [Holy] Spirit." The ongoing experience of being filled with the Spirit infuses us with everything we need to live like Jesus and bring God's will on earth as it is in heaven. Evangelist **Smith Wigglesworth** said,

> "I can never estimate what the baptism of the Holy Ghost has been to me... It is a luxury to be filled with the Spirit, and at the same time it is a divine command for us... I maintain that with a *constant filling* you will speak in tongues morning, noon and night. As you live in the Spirit, when you walk down the steps of the house where you live, the devil will have to go before you. You will be more than a conqueror over the devil.

> ...As you live in the spirit, you move, act, eat, drink, and do everything to the glory of God. Our message is always this, 'Be filled with the Spirit.' This is God's place for you, and it is as far above the natural life as the heavens are above the earth. Yield yourselves for God to fill."[4]

Peter, John, and the other disciples were all baptized in the Spirit at Pentecost. They were filled again with the Spirit during prayer shortly thereafter.

Carefully read this account in Acts 4:23-31. What can you learn from this account to help position yourself to be *ever filled* with the Spirit?

_____

_____

_____

_____

Through Paul, God says "do not neglect the gift" of the Holy Spirit, but "stir up that inner fire which God gave you" (1 Timothy 4:14; 2 Timothy 1:6 Phillips). In other words, be *continuously* filled with the Holy Spirit. Carefully read Ephesians 5:18-19; 6:18 and Jude 20. What is the Spirit showing you about keeping His fire stirred up in you?

_____

_____

_____

_____

> *So here's what I want you to do, God helping you: Take your everyday, ordinary life—your sleeping, eating, going-to-work, and walking-around life—and place it before God as an offering. Embracing what God does for you is the best thing you can do for him. Don't become so well-adjusted to your culture that you fit into it without even thinking. Instead, fix your attention on God. You'll be changed from the inside out.*
>
> —Romans 12:1-2 The Message

HE HAS GIFTED YOU FOR A PURPOSE

Each person is given something to do that shows who God is:
Everyone gets in on it, everyone benefits.

—1 Corinthians 12:7 The Message

The Holy Spirit has given us specific gifts to continue the work Jesus began. Although the gifts are diverse, "it is the one and only Spirit who distributes all these gifts. He alone decides which gift each person should have" (1 Corinthians 12:11 NLT).

Are these gifts for today? Should we be doing the works Jesus did? Absolutely. Evangelist **Reinhard Bonnke**, who has seen millions come to Christ across the African continent, declares,

> "I believe so strongly that God is the worker of miracles for His people. I believe the signs that followed Jesus as He walked the earth could—and should—be true in our lives today. Jesus said to His disciples, *He that believeth on me, the works that I do shall he do also; and greater works than these shall he do; because I go unto my Father."* [5]

Carefully read **Romans 12:3-8** and name the gifts mentioned. Overall, how would you describe these (their purpose and function)?

_____

_____

_____

_____

Now read **1 Corinthians 12:4-11** and identify the nine gifts. In general, how would you describe these (their purpose and function)?

_____

_____

_____

_____

Look over the gifts in both passages. Are any of these gifts operating in you? If so, which one(s)?

_____

_____

_____

_____

Are you unsure? Which of these gifts are you drawn to or excite you? Ask the Holy Spirit to show you how He has gifted you.

Your attitude toward others and how the Spirit has gifted you is important. God says, "Let Christ himself be your example as to what your attitude should be" (Philippians 2:5 Phillips). Reinhard confirms this, adding,

> "The success of the work of God does not depend on any of us…. It is all accomplished through dependence on Him. …I am a zero that God is able to use only because I value His voice above other voices. …Never should I see myself above another servant of God."[6]

Carefully read 1 Corinthians 12:12-26 and Romans 12:3-5. What is the Spirit showing you about your attitude? How important is each person's gift—including yours? What will happen to the Body of Christ if you neglect using your gift?

_____

_____

_____

_____

For Further Study…
Having the right attitude: Philippians 2:1-8; 2 Corinthians 8:9; Matthew 23:11-12
The Spirit also appoints believers to offices for a purpose: 1 Corinthians 12:28-31; Ephesians 4:11-14

LET HIM PRAY GOD'S WILL THROUGH YOU

God's Spirit is right alongside helping us along. If we don't know how or what to pray, it doesn't matter. He does our praying in and for us, making prayer out of our wordless sighs, our aching groans.

—Romans 8:26 The Message

Have you ever been so overwhelmed and broken by the circumstances of life that you didn't know what to pray? You're not alone. Countless saints have experienced this. In these moments, God wants you to *run to Him*, not from Him. Instead of clamming up, He wants you to open up. When you don't know what to say or how to pray, the Spirit of Christ living in you does.

It is vital that you know in your heart, not just your head, that God's Spirit is living in you. Take time to meditate on the following verses. What insights is the Holy Spirit revealing to you?

Meditate on Galatians 4:6; Romans 8:16; 1 Corinthians 6:19; John 14:23; 1 John 3:24; 4:12-13. Ask the Spirit to make Himself real to you.

_____

_____

_____

_____

God wants us to "pray in the Spirit at all times and on every occasion" (Ephesians 6:18 NLT). **Watchman Nee**, a dear minister who braved physical hardships and years of imprisonment, said,

> "Thank God, we have the almighty Holy Spirit to help us. We must rely on the indwelling Holy Spirit, who works within us with might, for He is our help in times of infirmity and ignorance. Though we do not know how to pray, even so, the indwelling Holy Spirit who himself knows the will of God, will teach us to pray according to the mind of God."[7]

Stop and think. How often do you really know how to pray for yourself, others, and the situations you're facing? What should be our attitude and approach to God in every prayer we pray?

Check out Proverbs 3:5-8; 28:26; Luke 18:9-14; James 4:6-10

Want to walk in God's perfect will? The Spirit will help bring it about by praying through you with cries, sighs, groans, and heavenly tongues. "And the Father who knows all hearts knows what the Spirit is saying, for the Spirit pleads for us believers in harmony with God's own will" (Romans 8:27 NLT). Carefully read this passage. What is the Spirit saying to you through this?

> For if you have the ability to speak in tongues, you will be talking only to God.... You will be speaking by the power of the Spirit, but it will all be mysterious. A person who speaks in tongues is strengthened personally.... For if I pray in tongues, my spirit is praying, but I don't understand what I am saying. Well then, what shall I do? I will pray in the spirit, and I will also pray in words I understand. I will sing in the spirit, and I will also sing in words I understand.
>
> —1 Corinthians 14:2, 4, 14-15 NLT

"As you surrender yourself to the Spirit, he will present you and your need before the Father's throne. The Holy Spirit knows the perfect mind and the perfect will of God. He who searches your heart and knows you better than you know yourself will bring that need before the throne of God, and you cannot miss when the Holy Spirit prays through you."

—Kathryn Kuhlman[8]

DISCUSSION QUESTIONS

If you are using this book as part of the Messenger Series on the Holy Spirit, please refer to video session 4.

1 | It is important to understand that there is a difference between the Holy Spirit coming to make His home in us at the time of salvation and the infilling of the Holy Spirit. How would you describe these two extraordinary experiences?

2 | Why do you think Jesus *commanded* His disciples to wait for the infilling of the Holy Spirit before moving forward to do anything for His kingdom (see Acts 1:4-5)? What can we learn from this principle of "waiting to receive power from on high," and how can we apply it in our lives today?

3 | The infilling of the Holy Spirit empowers us to speak in other *tongues*. A tongue is simply a language not recognizable to our understanding. Imagine you were one of the faithful Jews visiting Jerusalem from a foreign nation on the Day of Pentecost. How do you think you would have reacted to hearing the believers speak in your native tongue about salvation through Jesus Christ?

4 | When the Holy Spirit fills believers, what two dynamics are consistent in virtually every occurrence? For what reason did God most likely bring salvation and the infilling of the Holy Spirit to Cornelius and his family *simultaneously*? Share a story of how God broke out of a "religious box" you put Him in and expanded your understanding of who He is.

5 | If the manifestations of prophecy and speaking in tongues are for believers today, what did Paul mean when he said that *not all speak in tongues* (see 1 Corinthians 12:27-30) and that *tongues will cease* (see 1 Corinthians 13:8-12)? Read these verses carefully and explain.

6 | The Bible speaks of *four* kinds of tongues. Read the following passages
       and name the four categories of tongues, explaining why God has
       given these different manifestations of the Holy Spirit to His Church.
       1 Corinthians 14:22
       1 Corinthians 12:10
       1 Corinthians 14:14-15
       Romans 8:26-28

       Why is it important to understand the differences between these types
       of tongues?

7 | Can a believer be filled with the Holy Spirit and not speak in tongues?
       Why or why not? What are some common reasons this happens?

NOTES

CHAPTER SUMMARY:

- The empowerment of the Spirit is essential to all kingdom work.

- The infilling of the Holy Spirit is a separate experience that follows salvation.

- Salvation *repositions us in Christ*; the infilling of the Spirit *empowers us* to live like Him.

- Tongues have *not* ceased; they're in operation until we see Jesus face to face.

- There are four types of tongues: tongues as a sign for un-believers, tongues for interpretation, tongues for personal prayer, and tongues for intercession. The first two are for public use, and the second two are for private use.

5

The Spirit's Language

If you praise him in the private language of tongues, God understands you...
*for you are sharing **intimacies** just between you and him.*

—1 Corinthians 14:2 The Message

Day 1

I love how *The Message* portrays this personal encounter with our God. This expression of the *language of tongues* is a powerful interaction that occurs "just between you and [God]."

In the last chapter, we looked at the four types of tongues identified in the New Testament: tongues as a sign to unbelievers, tongues for interpretation in the church, tongues for personal prayer, and tongues for intercession. The first two types of tongues are intended for use in public ministry (among two or more people), while the latter two are private. In this chapter, we will continue examining the functions and nature of our *private* interactions with God's Spirit, which can include both speaking in tongues and speaking from the understanding. Together, these expressions comprise *the language of the Spirit.*

Again, to clarify: by referring to these expressions as "private," I do not mean that they are only to be used when a person is alone. Rather, private expressions in heavenly languages are used with sensitivity to the presence of those whom the Bible calls "uninformed" or "unbelievers." These expressions can occur when a person is alone or in the company of other believers who understand this manifestation of the Spirit. It is similar to the way I would have certain *private* conversations with my family that I wouldn't have in front of a group of recent acquaintances, for these new acquaintances would not understand what I was talking about (see 1 Corinthians 14:22-25 for more).

Notice that Paul refers to the use of tongues in 1 Corinthians 14:2 as a "private language." Sadly, many factions of the Church have misunderstood or completely dismissed the amazing gift of private tongues because they do not realize that intimacy requires an appropriate *time* and *place*.

There is a time and a place for a couple to enjoy intimacy. Is that time before they are married? No. Is that place in a public environment? Certainly not. What is beautiful and God-ordained in one setting can be tawdry and inappropriate in another. God intended for sexual intimacy to occur in private, only after the marriage vows have been exchanged. Likewise, certain types of tongues should only be expressed in private because their intended purpose is that of intimacy. The proper expression of spiritual intimacy, like that of physical intimacy, falls within a specific time and place. Should Christians abstain from the gift of sex because mankind has perverted God's original design and purpose for it? Of course not! In a similar fashion, we cannot discount or despise the gift of tongues.

I know that many in the Church have seen aspects of the gift of tongues misused or even abused. However, we must not refuse to educate the Body of Christ about this gift just because some have misunderstood or misappropriated it. That is why in this chapter, I want to explore the intimate nature of our heavenly language and help you develop a better understanding of its purpose and significance in our lives.

Remember, the Holy Spirit is the Spirit of truth. As you yield to the wisdom of God's Word, the Spirit will reveal *all* truth to you. Take a moment to pause and invite Him into this time of learning. Ask Him to remove from your mind any preconceived ideas or beliefs that are contrary to His Word. You can never experience the fullness of God if you allow your finite understanding to define and confine His infinite greatness.

The President and the King

As a citizen of the United States of America, I would be honored to receive an invitation to dine with our president. Our president is one of the most knowledgeable and powerful people on the face of the earth. Considering the numerous agencies at his disposal, there is very little information that he cannot obtain. The president's knowledge of our state of affairs would far exceed my own: he is the Commander-in-chief, whereas I am a citizen who does not hold a governmental office. Therefore, when discussing our nation's affairs, the president would have to talk to me on my level of understanding. If he didn't, I would not be able to relate to him, because successful communication requires common ground.

Similarly, when I communicate with the King of the universe, there is no way I can communicate with Him on His level. The U.S. president might know a lot about our country's state of affairs, but God knows everything. Nothing is hidden from Him. When I pray to God in my own understanding, I am limited to what I see and know. God wasn't satisfied to have this limited level of intimacy with His children. Therefore, He has made it possible for us to commune with Him *on His level*. He has done this through the gift of His Spirit. It's as if God said, "I don't want to merely communicate with My children on a level far below My knowledge, understanding, and wisdom. I want them to have the ability to go into deep fellowship with Me. So I'm going to give My children a Helper: My Spirit." The Holy Spirit's presence and communion make it possible for us to experience deep intimacy with the Creator.

God's will and ways surpass our limited understanding—but when we pray in the Spirit, we do not pray according to our own understanding. Instead, we pray according to the will of His Spirit. Did you catch that? When we pray in the Spirit, *we pray according to God's perfect will*!

A Language for War

For we do not wrestle against flesh and blood, but against the rulers, against the authorities, against the cosmic powers over this present darkness, against the spiritual forces of evil in the heavenly places. (Ephesians 6:12 ESV)

Sometimes it is easy for us to forget that Satan has declared an all-out war on humanity. His strategy has always been to separate us from our Creator, the One who is the very source of life. But God is aware of the enemy's ploys. In His infinite wisdom, God developed a secret strategy to thwart Satan's plans. Paul described this game-changer in 1 Corinthians 2:7-8: "The wisdom we speak of is the *mystery* of God—his plan that was previously hidden, even though he made it for our ultimate glory before the world began. But the rulers of this world have not understood it; if they had, they would not have crucified our glorious Lord" (NLT). Paul is describing the power of the cross, a *mystery* that "was previously hidden" but was revealed after Jesus died and was resurrected. Jesus' sacrifice on the cross made it possible for us to enter into a close relationship with God, thus thwarting our enemy's ancient plans.

God's plan for the cross is not the only mystery that was hidden from the rulers of this age. There are many aspects of God's wisdom (His Word) that have been hidden and can only be discovered and discerned by His Spirit. As believers, we have been granted access to these mysteries through communion with the Spirit. As I mentioned earlier in this book, God was not content merely to "save us." He also granted us position *in Christ* and entrusted us with authority and power over the same enemy who has long been the tormentor of our souls. We are now heirs and warriors in God's kingdom, and our purpose is to advance the cause of Christ. In His wisdom, God has created an avenue by which He can secretly communicate His perfect plan to those of us who fight for His cause.

In times of war, militaries will develop entire "languages" in order to furtively communicate plans and information. Often they develop complex codes and communicate over protected frequencies. Why do they do this? Secrecy is imperative to the safety of lives and the success of operations. If the enemy discovers their plans, he can plan an informed counterattack. As children of God, we have been given access to heaven's secret frequency through the Spirit—allowing us to discover the mysteries of God's strategies without exposing our Commander's plans to the enemy. Paul continues:

> Pray in the Spirit at all times and on every occasion. Stay alert
> and be persistent in your prayers for all believers everywhere.
> (Ephesians 6:18 NLT)

There is a reason God has commanded us to pray. As His warriors on earth, we are the ones who combat the forces of darkness. One of our most formidable weapons is praying in the Spirit. It keeps the enemy uniformed about the plans and purposes behind God's strategies.

At times God will move on the heart of a mother to begin interceding for her son. She may have no idea what's happening in her son's life, but she knows by the Spirit's urging to start praying. As she intercedes in her heavenly language, she is actually giving commands in the spiritual realm and praying God's perfect will over her son. For this reason we are told, "By wise counsel wage war" (Proverbs 20:18).

Our heavenly language transcends our understanding and is not limited by time or space. When we pray in the Spirit, we forsake our reliance on our own understanding and rely on the vastness of His infinite wisdom. This is one of the many reasons why Paul stated, "I wish you all spoke in tongues."

Our heavenly language is something that the enemy cannot decipher because it is an intimate exchange between God and His children; therefore, it is very effective in foiling the enemy's schemes against us and our fellow believers.

> Behold, I have given you authority…over all the power of the enemy. (Luke 10:19 ESV)

We believers have been equipped to forcefully advance the kingdom of God on the earth (see Matthew 11:12). The Church is the Body of Christ on the earth. As we have previously established, Jesus no longer physically resides here. We are the ambassadors and warriors of God's kingdom—we are the ones who carry and administer His transforming power to those in need of restoration, freedom, and redemption. But we can never be Christ's Body to a lost and dying world without the empowerment of His Spirit. Satan and his cohorts are not scared of you, but they are terrified of *who you are in Christ* and of *the power you wield* as a son or daughter of the Most High.

Day 2

A Language for Intimacy

My wife and I have been together long enough that we have developed our own little language. I can simply say, "CBOI," and my wife will know what I mean. You see, when we were first married, it seemed like every new ministry had "Outreach International" in its name. So Lisa and I decided to start Cuddle Bunny Outreach International (CBOI). We could look at each other and say, "CBOI," and we both knew that it was time for a hug or a kiss. Anyone else who heard us probably wondered, *What are you talking about?* It was a silly language, but it was an intimate language known only to Lisa and me. This is just one example of many intimate communication methods we have developed with each other.

Similarly, praying in our heavenly language enables us to intimately communicate with God. Someone might say, "But John, I don't understand what I'm praying. Doesn't the Bible even say, 'For if I pray in a tongue, my spirit prays, but my understanding is unfruitful' (1 Corinthians 14:14)?" Yes, that is true. But this is why the previous verse says, "Let him who speaks in a tongue pray that he may interpret" (verse 13). When I pray or commune with God in tongues, I ask Him to give me the interpretation of my prayers. Do you know what happens? Ideas, wisdom, and revelation come bubbling up out of my spirit. The best way I know how to describe it is that these insights bubble up like trapped air being released from the depths of the sea. They are released from deep within my inner man and surface in my mind or understanding.

Let me give an example. When I come across a scripture and think, *I don't understand that,* I will say, "Holy Spirit, teach me." Then I start praying in tongues. The revelation may not come right away; it usually comes later when I'm doing something like driving, taking a shower, just relaxing, or playing golf. All of sudden, it hits me! These revelations are the result of intimacy with the Spirit—I asked for His insight. God reveals His mysteries to the humble; as we humble ourselves (ask for the Spirit's guidance), we will experience deeper intimacy with Him and receive greater spiritual revelation.

The same is true of spiritual power. Paul wrote the following words spoken to him directly from God's Spirit:

> "My grace is sufficient for you, for my power [grace] is made
> perfect in weakness." Therefore I will boast all the more gladly
> of my weaknesses, so that the power of Christ may rest upon
> me. (2 Corinthians 12:9 ESV)

God's grace, which is His power, is also bestowed on those who are humble (which Paul refers to when he acknowledges his "weakness"). A greater measure of God's empowerment will rest upon you as you humble yourself by yielding to the infinite wisdom of His Spirit. This too is ultimately a byproduct of intimacy with the Spirit.

Our western society is results oriented. Oftentimes, if we don't see quick results for our efforts or investments, we lose our resolve. What we must understand is that when we pray in the Spirit, we are investing in the future. Sometimes it takes awhile before revelation bubbles up to the surface of our understanding. Praying in the Spirit requires faith because it begins where our natural understanding ends. It stretches our faith and increases our capacity to understand God's wisdom.

Praying with the Understanding

The focus of this chapter is praying in the Spirit; however, praying in the understanding is also extremely beneficial. Paul made it clear that we should pray in both the understanding and the Spirit.

I will pray with the spirit, and I will also pray with the understanding. I will sing with the spirit, and I will also sing with the understanding. (1 Corinthians 14:15)

When I pray in my understanding it directly edifies my mind. It evokes great emotion and passion. It connects me to whomever I am praying for: Lisa, my children, my friends, my staff, etc. Likewise, when I speak from my understanding to declare my Father's greatness, I am flooded with a sense of thanksgiving and gratitude.

There are also times when I pray in the understanding according to the Spirit's leading. This is actually another form of praying in the Spirit. But most often, I pray in the Spirit first, and then God gives me the interpretation or the understanding of what I just prayed. The words of understanding flow out of my mouth like a river.

As I write about the importance of praying in the Spirit, I am by no means belittling the need to pray in the understanding. I am instead hoping to communicate that a healthy prayer life includes both prayer in the Spirit and prayer from the understanding. Both are vital to our lives in God.

Our Life Source

Proverbs 20:27 says, "The spirit of man is the candle of the Lord, searching all the inward parts of the belly" (KJV). The wonders of God's Spirit are illuminated and initially revealed in our spirits, not in our minds. This is why, when we pray in the Spirit, we should also believe and ask for the interpretation. The revelation that the Holy Spirit gives to our spirits will then be released and rise to the surface of our understanding.

Proverbs 20:5 states, "Counsel [advice, wisdom, direction, purpose] in the heart of a man is like deep water, but a man [or woman] of understanding will draw it out." Through the power of the cross, God has given us a new heart (see Ezekiel 36:26). We are now able to draw out counsel (the Holy Spirit is called the Counselor) from the depths of our renewed hearts. Jesus' words in John 7:38-39 confirm this:

Anyone who believes in me may come and drink! For the Scriptures declare, "Rivers of living water will flow from *his heart.*" (When he said "living water," he was speaking of *the Spirit*, who would be given to everyone believing in him. But the Spirit had not yet been given, because Jesus had not yet entered into his glory.) (NLT)

This verse also brings to mind Isaiah 12:3:

With joy you will drink deeply from the fountain of salvation [living water]! (NLT)

John clearly stated that the "living water" Jesus said will flow from our hearts is "the Spirit." Why does Jesus liken the Spirit to water? Water conveys life and vitality; without it, life on earth would cease. By referring to the Spirit as "living water," Jesus is saying the Spirit is the very essence of life.

God says, "My people are destroyed for lack of knowledge" (Hosea 4:6). What knowledge is God talking about? God is specifically speaking of the knowledge of His ways and purpose. The amazing news is that God has sent His Spirit to us so that we can live in the fullness of life that comes with the knowledge of His heart.

It is impossible to serve God without first understanding who He is, even as my ministry team members cannot serve me well without first coming to know my heart. As we read God's Word and spend time in prayer, the Spirit reveals God's heart to us. This is the empowerment needed to live a joyful life. Nehemiah 8:10 states, "The joy of the Lord is your strength." In other words, when we delight in Him (experience the refreshment of His Spirit) we are given strength for what lies ahead. I don't know about you, but I never want to live a day without His joy.

The Mysteries of God

From these scriptures in Proverbs and John, we can see that the water springing forth from our hearts contains the mysteries or secret wisdom of God. We also know that God reveals these insights and mysteries by His Spirit. So now let's take another look at what Paul says in 1 Corinthians 2:7: "We speak the wisdom of God in a *mystery*."

The Greek word translated *mystery* does not mean "mysterious" or "ambiguous." It actually means "hidden or not fully manifested."[1]

Picture it like this: you are at a fancy restaurant. The chef comes to your table to ascertain your culinary preferences. He then customizes a meal to your particular tastes. When the meal is ready, a waiter comes and places your entrée in front of you. Because this is such a nice restaurant, the entrée remains covered until the time of its unveiling. You know what sits before you is your meal, but there is a certain mystery that still surrounds the dish.

When the time is right, the waiter says, "Voila!" and removes the cover from the dish. Now you're able to see the meal the chef crafted for you. It's not as if the meal did not exist before the cover was removed; the food was present even before you knew what it was. The waiter revealed the *mystery* of your dinner. The entrée was always known to the chef, but it was hidden from you until the cover was removed.

By His Spirit, God removes the cover from His hidden plan—His *mystery*. Through our partnership with the Spirit, we can now...

...speak the wisdom [or counsel] of God in a *mystery*...that we might know the things that have been freely given to us by God. These things we also speak, not in words which man's wisdom teaches but which the Holy Spirit teaches, comparing spiritual things with spiritual. (1 Corinthians 2:7, 12-13)

It was later in this same letter that Paul wrote, "For he who speaks in a tongue does not speak to men but to God, for no one understands him; however, in the spirit he speaks *mysteries*" (1 Corinthians 14:2). Do you see the correlation? When we speak in tongues, we speak the *mysteries* of God. We already know that these mysteries are hidden in the depths of our hearts (see Proverbs 20:5) and are drawn out when the living water of the Spirit's wisdom springs forth within us (see John 7:38-39). Therefore, praying in tongues edifies us because it draws out "living water," the very essence of life, so that we can understand the deepest counsel of the Spirit Himself!

As I mentioned earlier, there have been many times when I have encountered a scripture that surpasses my understanding. When this happens, I pray in the Spirit, and then the understanding follows. Numerous times I was in the process of writing a book when I suddenly hit a wall. It seemed I had nothing more to say. The only thing I can do when I reach a point like this is step away from my computer and start praying in tongues. When I do this, I often find myself overtaken by new revelation. What's happening in these moments? The living water of the Spirit of God is flowing from my heart!

If you are not in communion with God, then certain mysteries may continue to be hidden from your natural mind. These mysteries could include where you should go to church, who you should marry, which job you should take, which house you should buy, how to pray for your leaders, how to be a better spouse, how to handle a challenge you are facing with one of your children, how to excel in your job, and more. Aren't you glad that God did not leave us to simply fend for ourselves through our own understanding? Through His Spirit we can discover His plans (what's best) for our lives, and we will be able to enjoy His promised peace.

Day 3

Peace: A Gift of Intimacy

Galatians 5 tells us that peace is the evidence of the Spirit's presence and agreement in our lives. This is an amazing blessing with many practical applications in everyday life.

When I was a single man, the identity of my future wife was a mystery to me. At the time, I was dating a woman named Lisa Toscano. I knew I really liked her. I loved her personality and was very attracted to her. But I only wanted to marry the girl that God had selected for me. Lisa was living in Arizona, and I was in Texas. We both wanted God's direction regarding the future of our relationship. So I told Lisa, "Let's pray in the Spirit for thirty minutes every day for the next thirty days. Listen to your heart. If you feel a gnawing or uneasy feeling, then God is telling us not to go further in our relationship. But if you have a sense of peace, the Holy Spirit is encouraging us to take the next step in our relationship." As we prayed, we both individually sensed an overwhelming peace accompanied by anticipation and joy. After the thirty days, we discussed openly what we sensed while we were praying and discovered that we had both experienced the same things. We moved forward and were eventually married. It has been over thirty years, and I am so thankful both of us experienced that peace!

Romans 8:14 says, "For as many as are led by the Spirit of God, these are sons [and daughters] of God." The passage goes on to explain how the Spirit leads God's children: "The Spirit Himself *bears witness* with our spirit" (8:16). This is the primary way the Spirit leads us—by His peace or *witness*.

Have you ever wanted to do something that seemed like the right, logical decision, but every time you thought about it, you experienced a gnawing, uncomfortable feeling? You may have wondered, *What's wrong? Why do I feel this way? Everything about this decision seems right.* If you were in communion with the Holy Spirit, that uncomfortable feeling was Him telling you, "Don't move in that direction." I have experienced this many times. Sometimes my decision to follow the Spirit's leading does not make sense until years down the road. I have learned to trust Him in these instances. Remember, His wisdom is not limited to time or space, which means He is always considering your future as He guides your present.

Then there are other times when I have felt a great peace surrounding a decision that seemed like a huge risk. That was the peace of Christ ruling in my heart. Hear the words of the Apostle Paul:

And let the peace (soul harmony which comes) from Christ rule (act as umpire continually) in your hearts [deciding and settling with finality all questions that arise in your minds, in that peaceful state] to which as [members of Christ's] one body you were also called [to live]. (Colossians 3:15 AMP)

I love how the *Amplified* version likens the Holy Spirit to an umpire. A good umpire makes his calls without any second thought. Likewise, the Holy Spirit will decisively settle all questions (decisions, concerns, etc.) that arise in your mind. He will share His wisdom with you if you allow Him to make the calls. Many times His "call" is communicated through a peace that transcends human understanding; this is the witness of the Spirit. Scripture says,

And the peace of God, which surpasses all understanding,
will guard your hearts and minds through Christ Jesus.
(Philippians 4:7)

We have been positioned *in Christ Jesus*, which means we have access to the peace that is so elusive in our day and age. Jesus is the Prince of Peace, so those who are in Him have been promised peace. When we invite the Holy Spirit into our decision-making processes, He will always bear witness through the peace of Christ Jesus.

Peace and Decision Making

As the leader of Messenger International, I have made many decisions that were solely affirmed by His peace. The objective in question may have seemed impossible, but God's peace kept me from limiting Messenger International's potential to my own understanding.

There have been times when I have clearly heard the Spirit speak to me. As I was preparing to write this book, for instance, I was actually planning to write on an entirely different subject. During a time of prayer and fasting, the Holy Spirit instructed me to instead write about the wonder of who He is.

Most of my decisions are guided by the peace of God (always in agreement with His Word), not by a clear directive. However, there have been certain times when God's Spirit has spoken to me. I find this usually occurs when God is establishing a completely new direction for me. Let me give you an example.

Messenger International's primary goal is to build the local church. We believe that the local church is God's most strategic way of reaching the lost, bringing hope and provision to those in need, and making disciples of the nations. More than 20,000 churches in North America have used our curriculums. For many years, our main focus was to reach churches in the United States, Canada, Australia, and the United Kingdom.

Then on May 31, 2010, God spoke to me as I was reading the book of Daniel: "You've been faithful in reaching out to the local church in the English-speaking world. Now I'm sending you to the entire realm—the nations of the world." It was a *wow* moment. I had no idea how this was going to happen. So I called a meeting with the directors of our ministry. I shared the vision that God had placed in my heart and told them that during the course of 2011, I wanted to give away 250,000 books to leaders in developing nations. Everyone was shocked. We had never given away anything close to this number of books in a single year. My Chief Operating Officer and other department heads questioned me repeatedly over this mandate. My COO finally asked if I would bring this objective to God in prayer.

I had clearly heard from God that we were to reach out to pastors and leaders all over the world, but God had not specifically told me that the first step toward this goal was to give away 250,000 books during the coming year. So I took this goal to Him in prayer. Sure enough, I had a peace. The Holy Spirit did not have to audibly speak to me because I knew this goal was in line with His original directive. I felt His *witness* with it. When I reported this to the team, they immediately got behind the vision. Sure enough, God moved in miraculous ways, and we were able to give away more than 270,000 books to pastors and leaders in 47 nations that year.

In 2011, I met with an Iraqi pastor in Beirut, Lebanon (I was in the

Middle East speaking to 2,500 pastors and leaders). He led the largest church in his city and was a young man of thirty-six years. He told me, "Mr. Bevere, you are like a father to me. I've read as many of your books as I could get my hands on. I've even used my credit card to download resources from your website."

When he said that, I wanted to crawl into a hole. Here was a man from a war-torn nation with very little finances doing everything he could to get Messenger International's materials. It caused me to once again cry out to God for wisdom on how to help these local churches by empowering their leaders. By praying in the Spirit, I received an idea for how we could give pastors in developing nations not only books but entire curriculums. The next year, we gave 1.3 million resources to these pastors and leaders. That number has continued to multiply ever since.

A critical piece of the puzzle that came by praying in the Spirit was CloudLibrary.org, a website that allows these pastors and leaders, along with their congregations, to download resources in their native languages free of charge. So what was in excess of 270,000 resources given away in 2011 now multiplies in its reach month by month! This is the kind of work God is able to do in and through us when we follow the Holy Spirit's *witness* of peace!

Day 4

Receiving Direction

An area that seems to trouble the greatest number of believers is finding God's direction. I often hear people say, "I don't know what God wants me to do with my life!" James tells us what to do if we need direction: "If any of you lacks wisdom, let him ask of God" (1:5). The Greek word for wisdom is *sophia*, which is more fully described as "the capacity to understand and, as a result, to act wisely."[2] Think of it like this: through God's wisdom we can first understand and *then* act.

Who gives us the capacity to understand God's wisdom and put it into practice? The Holy Spirit. I have been in circumstances in which I really needed direction. When I began praying in tongues, God's wisdom and direction arose from my spirit and entered my understanding. The act of praying in tongues illuminates God's direction for our lives.

Let's read Proverbs 20:5 again. It says, "Counsel in the heart of man is like deep water, but a man [or woman] of understanding will draw it out." Other English translations use the word *purpose* instead of *counsel*. In Christ, you have been granted an assignment, or purpose, that is unique to you. This purpose will determine your direction, and it is hidden deep in your heart. As you pray in the Spirit and discover God's counsel, He will reveal your purpose. This will not happen overnight, so be patient. As you spend time in God's Word and in prayer, He will reveal your purpose to you. One of my sons likes to put it this way: the Bible is our map and the Spirit is our Guide.

This gift of direction is available in every area of your life. If you are having a hard time with one of your children, take a step back and make time to pray in the Spirit. He will show you how to respond. If you are in sales and you don't know what to do, close your office door and ask for insight from the One who knows everything. He already resides in you; now simply draw out what has not yet been revealed to you. His desire is to give you direction! Isaiah 48:17 says, "I am the Lord your God, Who teaches you to profit, Who leads you by the way you should go." God wants you to live out your kingdom purpose, and He desires to lead you every step of the way.

I sometimes hear people say, "John, that's just 'spiritual' and kind of weird. We can't really bring these types of requests to God. He only cares about ministry-related things." First of all, there is nothing weird about God, so there is nothing weird about His involvement in any and every area of our lives. People may be weird, but God is never weird. Also, we should never discount God's promise just because certain people have perverted or misused an expression of His Spirit.

Secondly, the Bible instructs us to "pray without ceasing" (1 Thessalonians 5:17). Many Christians have never studied the context of this verse to understand what it means. Obviously, Paul is not saying, "Keep your lips moving in prayer every minute of the day." After all, the Bible tells us to share the gospel and encourage one another. We cannot do either of these things if we spend every second moving our lips in prayer.

What Paul is actually referring to in this verse is *continuous communion with the Spirit of God*. How can we experience this? Paul tells us the answer, for he goes on to say: "Do not quench the Spirit" (verse 19). To pray without ceasing is to never quench the Holy Spirit's presence. It means that you are aware of His presence and sensitive to His voice. In other words, don't suppress His involvement in your life. The Spirit wants to be involved in every aspect of your life. He wants to guide you. His desire is to have constant communion with you. This unceasing communion will produce His peace, strength, and direction in your life.

I'm not called to be a businessman. But if I were, I would spend a lot of time praying in the Spirit about my business. I would then make decisions according to the peace in my heart. Don't ever discredit your ability to receive direction from your Creator just because you are not in "full-time ministry." He guides your path, just as He guides mine.

Personal Times of Prayer

I find that my prayer time is so much more effective when I begin it by first reading Scripture. The Word of God clears my mind and seems to open the channel from my spirit to my intellect. After this time of reading, I am much more connected with the Holy Spirit, and my time of prayer is enriched by His manifest presence.

I have also learned that God is quick to reveal Himself when I intentionally honor His presence in my life. When I start meditating on His greatness and goodness, all of a sudden the Holy Spirit reveals Himself. Why? The psalmist gives us the answer: "God is...to be held in reverence by all those around Him" (Psalm 89:7). If you want to experience God's presence, you must approach Him with reverence. The quickest way to squelch the presence of God is to dishonor Him by taking His Spirit for granted.

When Jesus modeled prayer for His disciples (including us), He began by saying, "Our Father in heaven, hallowed be Your name" (Matthew 6:9). In other words, when we approach our Father, we must first enter His presence with holy reverence. When we do, the Holy Spirit will manifest His presence, for He knows that He is being held in reverence. His presence will give us perspective, wisdom, knowledge, and power. He truly is our life source! Why would we ever want to separate ourselves from Him?

Interceding in the Spirit

I used to regularly pray with a particular pastor friend of mine. During our times of prayer, we would often intercede in tongues. One time we knew we were speaking and giving directives to some area in the Middle East. The next day we found out that there had been a massive earthquake in Turkey. I believe my friend and I were interceding for that nation. We were connected with them through the Spirit, because the same Spirit resides in all of us. God was speaking His will for those in Turkey through us.

This act of spiritual intercession is extremely significant in the advancement of God's kingdom on the earth. The enemy hates that we can declare the will of God over our distant brothers and sisters. His goal is to divide and separate the Church, and he would love to limit our intercession to what we know by our own understanding.

Perhaps you have never realized how closely connected you are to other believers worldwide. It is entirely possible for you to accurately intercede for believers in other lands, even if you have no natural contact with them.

I once met a man from the Masai tribe while I was in Kenya. He later visited the United States and stayed with some friends of mine in Pennsylvania. The gentleman stayed with them for over a month. On several occasions, he updated his hosts on the status of his family back in Africa. Finally, the hostess said, "How do you know what's going on with your family? They do not have access to any telephones." He replied, "Paul knew what was going on with the Colossian and Corinthian churches when he was far away from them. As I pray in the Spirit, the Lord shows me what's going on with my family members." The verses he was referring to were Colossians 2:5: "For though I am absent in the flesh, yet I am with you in spirit, rejoicing to see your good order," and 1 Corinthians 5:3: "Even though I am not with you in person, I am with you in the Spirit" (NLT). Paul was connected with the people of those churches in the Spirit and knew about their affairs and proceedings without being physically present among them.

There have been many times when I know one of my team members or partners has been praying for me. I will be in the midst of grave and dangerous circumstances when God suddenly and miraculously intervenes. I know in these instances that someone was praying protection over me and interceding for me in the Spirit.

Experiencing Rest

Brethren, do not be children in understanding…. In the law
it is written: "With men of other tongues and other lips I will
speak to this people." (1 Corinthians 14:20-21)

As you have probably figured out by now, Paul writes a lot about
tongues in 1 Corinthians 14. In these verses, Paul is actually paraphras-
ing the words of Isaiah; for in Isaiah 28:11-12, we read:

For with stammering lips and another tongue He will speak to
this people, to whom He said, "This is the *rest* with which you
may cause the weary to rest," And, "This is the *refreshing*."

God prophesied through Isaiah that speaking in tongues would
provide rest and refreshing. Once, one of my friends who pastors a large
church was talking to the pastor of another large church. The pastor of
the second church told my friend, "I'm ready to leave the ministry. I'm
tired. I'm weary. I'm worn out."

My friend responded, "You've stopped praying in the Holy Spirit,
haven't you?"

The other pastor stammered, "Well…"

My friend continued, "How much time do you spend praying in the
Spirit?"

The other pastor was still hesitant but eventually said, "Well, I'm
constantly preparing my messages, and I've got a lot of things going on
with my 15,000-member church, and…"

My friend asked again, "Are you praying in the Spirit?"

Finally, the other pastor responded, "No, to be really honest with
you, I'm not."

My friend said, "Start praying in the Spirit."

Soon enough, the once-weary pastor no longer wanted to resign from the ministry. Today, both he and his church are thriving!

Why was it so important for the pastor to pray in tongues? We receive supernatural rest and rejuvenation when we pray in the Spirit.

How can Dr. Cho lead a church of over 800,000 people and never get burnt out? He prays in the Spirit. I can't think of a pastor who experiences more pressure and responsibility than Dr. Cho. His church has completely transformed South Korea, and he is one of the most respected pastors in the world. It would be impossible for any man or woman to bear this weight in their own abilities. But I know that Dr. Cho doesn't rely on his own understanding. He prioritizes his times of prayer and prays in the Spirit for hours every day. This time of prayer provides him with great strength and rest.

Lester Sumrall was a great man of God. I had the privilege of spending time with him on several occasions. Doctor Sumrall slept only four hours a night and would write four books at the same time! He had much more energy than his staff members (who were half his age) and many younger preachers. Where did he find this strength? He spent a lot of time praying in the Spirit.

Please understand, we should never abuse our bodies. God clearly commands us to honor and keep the Sabbath. We should all enjoy physical rest. I play golf because it takes me away from work and refreshes my mind and body. It is a great source of rest for me. But along with the observance of Sabbath rest, praying in the Spirit will refresh our bodies and souls. Unfortunately, many people have experienced burn out prematurely because they were not finding rest in the Spirit.

Our Inner Man

He who speaks in a tongue edifies himself. (1 Corinthians 14:4)

The Greek word for *edifies* is *oikodomeo*. This word literally means "to construct or build."[3] When we pray in the Spirit, we build up our capacity to house the presence and power of God. Jesus used this same Greek word when He said, "Everyone who hears these words of mine and puts them into practice is like a wise man who *built* [*oikodomeo*] his house on the rock" (Matthew 7:24 NIV).

Similarly, God says to us through Jude,

But you, beloved, building yourselves up on your most holy faith, praying in the Holy Spirit. (Jude 20)

I remember a time when one of my friends had a son who was very sick. The doctors could not figure out what was wrong with the boy, and my friend did not know what to do. Finally, he went into his office and prayed in the Spirit for five hours. He walked out of his office, drove home, and went straight to his son's bedroom. With great authority, he told his son to get out of bed. The boy was completely healed from that moment on. What had happened? Those hours of praying in the Spirit had increased my friend's capacity to intercede for and minister to his son. Everything we receive from God, we receive by faith. There simply is no other way. Time with the Spirit actually increases our ability to receive the promises and manifest presence of God because it edifies our inner man.

Deeper Worship

Praying in our heavenly language gives us the ability to worship and praise God on a deeper level. Paul said:

> Otherwise, if you bless with the spirit, how will he who occupies the place of the uninformed say "Amen" at your giving of thanks, since he does not understand what you say? For *you indeed give thanks well*. (1 Corinthians 14:16-17)

Paul is addressing corporate expressions of praise and pointing out that when we "bless with the Spirit" (praise God in tongues), we do our fellow man no benefit. Because praising in tongues is a private expression, it brings personal edification but not group edification. Paul is not devaluing the act of praising God in tongues. He is simply saying that there is a time and a place for it.

Notice how Paul concludes his point: "For you indeed give thanks well"! When we praise God in tongues, we allow the Spirit to beautifully extol the wonders and mysteries of God through us. There is a deeper level of worship that occurs when we praise God in a heavenly tongue. This is why Paul sang both in the Spirit and in the understanding (see 1 Corinthians 14:15).

Anyone Can Be Filled with the Spirit

It grieves my heart when Christians look down upon other believers because they do not speak or pray in tongues. These brothers and sisters in Christ simply have not experienced this amazing gift of the Spirit. They are not to be shamed or belittled, for we are all one in Christ.

As we discussed in the last chapter, the gift of speaking in tongues is available to every believer; those who do not yet speak in tongues have not been excluded from this promise. Jesus said, "These signs *will* follow those who believe…they will speak with new tongues" (Mark 16:17). Paul said, "I wish you *all* spoke with tongues" (1 Corinthians 14:5). God's heart is for all of His children to enjoy the amazing benefits of our heavenly language.

How Does One Receive the Holy Spirit?

Before I continue, let me first note that many of my friends have received the infilling of the Spirit in the car, at home, and even at their offices. All we have to do is ask, and our heavenly Father will give us His Spirit. If you have already asked for this gift, you must simply learn how to yield.

First and foremost, before you can receive the infilling of the Holy Spirit, you must receive Jesus Christ as your Lord and Savior. Jesus said that the world (those who have not received salvation) cannot receive the Holy Spirit (see John 14:17). If you have not made Jesus the Lord of your life, you can submit yourself to His lordship right now. (For more on how to receive salvation, see the Appendix.)

If you are already a child of God, you may still be hindered from enjoying the infilling of the Spirit if there is a *deliberate*—intentional—pattern of disobedience in your life. God gives the Holy Spirit "to those who obey Him" (Acts 5:32). This does not mean that you have to be perfect. It simply means that you must humble yourself before Him. This is a sign of surrender to His will. As you humble yourself, God will give you His grace to overcome the snares of sin, and you will once again be open to receive the infilling of the Spirit.

One of the greatest snares of disobedience in the lives of many believers is offense. You must be intentional to forgive those who have wronged you. Without exception, I have witnessed that as soon as an offended believer who wants to receive the infilling of the Spirit extends forgiveness, the Spirit will manifest. Take a moment right now to release those who have wronged you and ask God to give you His heart for them. (I discuss the issue of offense in much greater detail in my book *The Bait of Satan*.)

Simply Ask in Faith...

If a son asks for bread from any father among you, will he give him a stone? Or if he asks for a fish, will he give him a serpent instead of a fish? Or if he asks for an egg, will he offer him a scorpion? If you then, being evil, know how to give good gifts to your children, how much more will your heavenly Father give the Holy Spirit to those who ask Him! (Luke 11:11-13)

Some have taught that when you ask for the Holy Spirit, you might receive an evil spirit instead. These words from Jesus should alleviate this fear entirely. God is the giver of every *good* and *perfect* gift (see James 1:17). If you ask the Father for the Holy Spirit, He is not going to give you a demon. He will give you His Spirit. So do not be afraid to open yourself to the infilling of His Spirit.

Once you have opened yourself to the Spirit, do not expect the Holy Spirit to grab your tongue and force you to speak. He has given you a free will. The Spirit is a gentleman who will never push you. Satan will push you; the Holy Spirit will guide or lead you. The Spirit will give you the words (it may begin with syllables, sounds, or stammering fragments of words), but you must yield to Him in three areas: your lips, your tongue, and your vocal chords. As you do, a heavenly language will start bubbling up from your spirit like a percolator. It may only be one syllable at first. But as you yield by faith to speak that syllable, more will continue to come. Again, everything is received from God by faith. The gift of tongues is no different. Just speak what He gives you by faith, and though you may begin with a stammering lip, what you utter will eventually become a fully developed language.

Greater Levels

The reason I spent the majority of the last two chapters discussing the gift of tongues is that I believe God wants us to have a heavenly language that connects us more deeply to Him and unites His people for His kingdom purposes. The Holy Spirit's passion (His desire) is for all men and women to know Jesus. As we grow in intimacy and partnership with Him, He will lift up our eyes and reveal the world to us in a new light. We will see a world in desperate need of Christ, but we will also see and know by His Spirit how we can play our part in making Christ known.

I hope you have enjoyed this introduction to the Spirit of God. All that you have learned in these chapters is truly a small taste of His infinite, eternal, matchless wonder—and He longs to take you to greater levels every single day of your life. I encourage you to read this book again from time to time so that the Spirit can quicken your heart to know Him in new and deeper ways.

The Holy Spirit delights in revealing Jesus to you. Honor His presence and invite Him into every area of your life, not just the "spiritual" ones. He has promised never to leave you or forsake you—enjoy that amazing promise every minute of every day. As you read God's Word and spend time in His presence, you will come to know the Spirit more and more intimately. The exciting news is that it is an endless journey. There will always be more that He longs to reveal to you. Don't settle for what you've heard, seen, or known. Challenge the limits of your understanding by allowing the Spirit of Jesus Christ to rule your life. As you do, I believe that you will see the glory and majesty of God displayed in your world like never before.

Praying in the Spirit...

OPENS THE DOOR TO DEEPER INTIMACY

If you praise him in the private language of tongues, God understands you...for you are sharing intimacies just between you and him.

—1 Corinthians 14:2 The Message

The greatest blessing of praying in the language of the Spirit is greater intimacy with God. The Lord of all creation desires fellowship and communion with us so much that He put His own Spirit in our spirits, empowering us to communicate with Him on His level. How amazing! Pastor **Kenneth Hagin, Sr.,** stated,

> "God is a Spirit. When we pray in tongues, our spirit is in direct contact with God, who is a Spirit. We are talking to Him by a divine supernatural means. ...Speaking with other tongues is not only the *initial* evidence of the Holy Spirit's infilling, but is a *continual* experience for the rest of one's life. For what purpose? To assist us in the worship of God.
>
> Continuing to pray and worship God in tongues helps us to be ever conscious of His indwelling presence. If I can be conscious of the indwelling presence of the Holy Ghost every day, it is bound to affect the way I live."[1]

When we pray in the Spirit, we do not pray in *our* understanding, but in God's understanding. His Spirit prays the perfect will of God through us!

It is important to pray in the Spirit and feed on God's Word everyday, for this is how we intimately connect with Him. What is your daily time and place to commune with God? How has the Spirit shown you His deep, personal love?

_____

_____

_____

If you don't have a time and place, pray and ask the Holy Spirit *when* and *where* He would like to meet and to demonstrate His deep love for you.

Have you disregarded or despised the gift of speaking in tongues? If so, why? How is this lesson helping you see the language of the Spirit in a more positive, powerful light?

_____

_____

_____

_____

If you have disregarded or despised the gift of tongues, ask God to forgive you and to fill you afresh with His Spirit.

Some have struggled with using their prayer languages because they only have one or two words. Does this apply to you? If so, imagine the Spirit gently speaking these words to you: *"I love you. Will you use what I have given you? Will you love and honor Me by speaking the words you have? Though they are few, they are special between you and me."* Take a moment and respond.

_____

_____

_____

_____

Don't compare your intimate language of prayer to that of others. Steward the words the Spirit has given you. As you are faithful with little, He will give you more to steward! **Check out** Matthew 25:14-23, paying close attention to verses 20-23.

Praying in the Spirit…
UNLOCKS THE MYSTERIES OF GOD

Knowledge about the mysteries of the kingdom of heaven has been given to you. …Those who understand these mysteries will be given more knowledge, and they will excel in understanding them....

—Matthew 13:11-12 GW

Jesus said you have been given the chance to understand the secrets and mysteries of His kingdom. How do you receive and understand these secrets? By abiding in relationship with His Spirit. God's mysteries are revealed as you pray in the Spirit and spend time with Him.

Oswald Chambers was an author, speaker, and champion of intimate devotion to God. In the well-known book *My Utmost for His Highest*, he says:

"What is the sign of a friend? That he tells you secret sorrows? No, that he tells you *secret joys*. Many will confide to you their secret sorrows, but the last mark of intimacy is to confide secret joys."[2]

What is one of the most amazing mysteries of God that the Spirit has revealed to you? Why is it special?

_____

_____

_____

Do you share *your* personal thoughts, feelings, and desires with the Spirit? Do you ever talk with Him about your greatest dreams or fears? Friends tell. Pause and share something intimate with Him—something dear to your heart that you have not shared before or haven't mentioned for a long time.

_____

_____

_____

If you don't intimately share things with the Spirit, why? Ask Him to show you what is hindering you and to help you freely share your heart.

Communicating with God is not just speaking; it's also *listening*. A balance of the two is needed. If we don't take time to listen, we can't hear what the Spirit is saying. Chambers continues:

> "Have we ever let God tell us any of His joys, or are we telling God our secrets so continually that we leave no room for Him to talk to us? At the beginning of our Christian life we are full of requests to God, then we find that God wants us to get into relationship with Himself, to get us in touch with His purposes. Are we so wedded to Jesus Christ's idea of prayer—'Thy will be done'—that we catch the secrets of God?"[3]

God says there is a time for everything, which includes a time to speak and a time to be silent in prayer (see Ecclesiastes 3:1-7). Ask the Spirit, "Am I always talking during prayer? Do I give You time to reveal Your mysteries? Have You been trying to tell me something that I have not been quiet enough to hear? If so, what is it?" Be still and listen. What is the Holy Spirit speaking to you?

_____

_____

_____

_____

This is my prayer. That God…will give you spiritual wisdom and the insight to know more of him: that you may receive that inner illumination of the spirit which will make you realise how great is the hope to which he is calling you—the magnificence and splendour of the inheritance promised to Christians—and how tremendous is the power available to us who believe in God.

—Ephesians 1:17-19 Phillips

Praying in the Spirit...
PRODUCES PEACE WITHIN

But the Holy Spirit produces this kind of fruit in our lives: ...peace....
—Galatians 5:22 NLT

What is peace? Sometimes knowing what something is *not* helps us know what it truly is. True peace, the peace that Jesus gives through His Spirit, is *not* about having a full bank account, perfect health, a beautiful home and extravagant possessions, or relationships that are void of conflict.

True peace—God's peace—is not defined by external circumstances or conditions. It is stability in the midst of difficulty. It is the ability to remain mentally, emotionally, physically, and spiritually calm and collected in the midst of problems.

Stop and ask yourself, *What is my understanding of peace? What is my peace anchored in? How does my understanding of peace differ from the true peace of the Spirit? What needs to change?*

_____

_____

_____

_____

Through the sacrifice of Christ, we are given peace *with* God. Through the infilling of the Holy Spirit, we are given the peace of God. Jesus Himself said,

> "I leave behind with you—peace; I give you **my own peace** and my gift is nothing like the peace of this world. You must not be distressed and you must not be daunted."
>
> —John 14:27 Phillips

What are we to do with the peace given to us by the Prince of Peace?

*And let the peace (soul harmony which comes) from Christ rule (**act as umpire continually**) in your hearts [deciding and settling with finality all questions that arise in your minds, in that peaceful state] to which as [members of Christ's] one body you were also called [to live].*

—Colossians 3:15 AMP

Imagine yourself as the batter who has stepped up to home plate. Behind you squats the *Umpire of Peace*, and each ball the pitcher throws is a decision you need to make. Now carefully reread Colossians 3:15. How important are the umpire's calls? What is the Holy Spirit speaking to you about allowing Him to be your Umpire of Peace?

_____

_____

_____

_____

The primary way the Spirit leads us into God's perfect will is through a sense of peace within. This is what Scripture means when it says "the Spirit Himself bears witness with our spirit" (Romans 8:16). What decisions are you facing right now that you need God to lead you in? Pause and pray in the Spirit. Then wait for His witness of peace. What is He speaking to you?

_____

_____

_____

_____

Praying in the Spirit...
RELEASES WISDOM AND DIRECTION

If you want to know what God wants you to do, ask him, and he will gladly tell you, for he is always ready to give a bountiful supply of wisdom to all who ask him; he will not resent it.

—James 1:5 TLB

Who is the Giver of wisdom and direction? The Holy Spirit. Isaiah calls Him the Spirit of wisdom and understanding, the Spirit of knowledge, and the Spirit of counsel. Jesus said He is our Teacher who guides us into all truth. Where does our Teacher live? Inside us—His temple. Whenever you lack wisdom on what to do, pray with your understanding and *in the Spirit*, and He will give you the direction you need!

Take time to ponder these powerful promises, remembering the Lord and the Spirit are the same.

> This is what the Lord says...″I am the Lord your God, who teaches you what is good for you and leads you along the paths you should follow.″
>
> —Isaiah 48:17 NLT

> Whether you turn to the right or to the left, your ears will hear a voice behind you, saying, "This is the way; walk in it."
>
> —Isaiah 30:21 NIV84

> I [the Lord] will instruct you and teach you in the way you should go; I will counsel you with My eye upon you.
>
> —Psalm 32:8 AMP

> The Friend, the Holy Spirit whom the Father will send at my request, will make everything plain to you.
>
> —John 14:26 The Message

> When the Spirit of truth comes, he will guide you into all truth.
>
> —John 16:13 NLT

Show me the path where I should go, O Lord; point out the right road for me to walk. Lead me; teach me; for you are the God who gives me salvation. I have no hope except in you. ...He will teach the ways that are right and best to those who humbly turn to him. ... Where is the man who fears the Lord? God will teach Him how to choose the best.

—Psalm 25:4-5, 9, 12 TLB

What do you need wisdom and direction for? Is it your job? Your health? Your marriage? Your children? Your finances? Your friendships? Whatever the situation, try walking out these steps:

1. *Make your specific request for wisdom* known to God, thanking Him for His direction in the past (see Philippians 4:6-7).

2. *Pray in the Spirit.* Use the gift of tongues to pray as long and as passionately as the Spirit desires to pray through you (see Ephesians 6:18; Romans 8:26-27).

3. *Ask the Spirit for the interpretation.* He will reveal the mystery of what you just prayed (see 1 Corinthians 14:13).

4. *Write what He reveals* (realizing it may not come immediately, but it will come).

5. *Ask the Holy Spirit for grace* to act on the direction He gives.

My greatest need for wisdom and direction is

This is the wisdom and direction the Holy Spirit is giving me:

Praying in the Spirit...
STRENGTHENS AND BUILDS YOU UP

A person who speaks in tongues is strengthened personally...

—1 Corinthians 14:4 NLT

Why does the enemy fight so hard to keep you from praying in tongues? First Corinthians 14:4 gives a powerful reason: he doesn't want you to be strengthened. The stronger you are in spirit, the stronger you are for Christ—and the greater threat you are to Satan's kingdom.

Just as your car's alternator recharges your battery, praying in the Spirit recharges your spirit. It drives away fear, depression, and negativity. It builds you up in ways that cannot be expressed. When you pray in tongues, you increase your capacity to house the presence and power of God.

Are you *regularly* or *rarely* praying in the Spirit? If regularly, *how often* and *for how long*? If rarely, why?

What happens *inside you* when you invest time into praying in tongues? What other fruit and manifestations of the Spirit have you witnessed as a result? How do these encourage you to pray?

How do you usually respond to stressful, draining situations? Have you tried praying in the Spirit? Pause and pray, "Holy Spirit, change my natural, negative response into the supernatural, positive response of praying in tongues. Fill me with You like never before!"

What actions is the Holy Spirit telling you to take that will make Him a greater part of your everyday life? Write them down, and put them into practice.

No doubt, the enemy has brought thoughts to your mind and stirred up feelings in your flesh to keep you from praying in tongues. He does this to most believers. Below are some of the common reasons and excuses he offers. Sound familiar? Write down any others you can think of; then pray and ask the Holy Spirit for a God-empowered reply to every lie the enemy brings.

That's not God; you made that up.

_____

I feel/sound so silly.

_____

You're just repeating what somebody else said.

_____

This doesn't do any good.

_____

I just don't feel like praying in tongues.

_____

All I have is a word or two.

_____

What would so-and-so think if they heard me?

_____

_____

Friend, don't let the enemy dupe you into thinking you shouldn't pray in tongues. Cast down his thoughts and push past those feelings. Open your mouth daily and "carefully build yourselves up in this most holy faith by praying in the Holy Spirit" (Jude 20 The Message).

DISCUSSION QUESTIONS

If you are using this book as part of the Messenger Series on the Holy Spirit, please refer to video session 5.

1 | Praying in tongues (the language of the Spirit) is extremely beneficial. Take a few minutes to name as many of the benefits as you can remember. Of these, which is most valuable to you at this time in your life? If you feel comfortable, share why.

2 | One reason God has given us the gift of tongues is to keep the enemy from knowing what's going on. God is all-knowing; Satan is not. Satan does not understand the divine frequency of the Spirit's language. Share any specific incident(s) when you prayed in tongues (interceded) and overcame the devil's plans in your life or the lives of others.

Leaders: Scriptures to consider: Luke 10:19; Ephesians 6:10-18; 2 Corinthians 10:3-5; Matthew 11:12; Revelation 12:11.

> *Pray in the Spirit at all times and on every occasion. Stay alert and be persistent in your prayers for all believers everywhere.*
>
> —Ephesians 6:18 NLT

3 | When we need wisdom on what to do in a situation, praying in the Holy Spirit is a vital key to receiving divine direction. Carefully read Proverbs 20:5; 1 Corinthians 14:13 and John 7:38-39. Describe how praying in tongues releases God's counsel, which has been deposited within our hearts.

4 | Abiding in communion with the Person of the Holy Spirit allows hidden "mysteries" to be revealed. These mysteries include things like where we should go to church, who we should marry, which job we should take, which house we should buy, how to pray for others, how to be a better spouse or parent, and how to deal with difficulties at work. If you're willing, share with the group how praying in the Spirit has unlocked the answers to one or more of these situations for you.

5 | In 1 Corinthians 14:15, we see that there is value in both praying in the Spirit and praying with the understanding. What are some benefits of praying with the understanding? How does praying in the Spirit help us pray more accurately in our understanding?

6 | First Thessalonians 5:17 instructs us to "pray without ceasing." Does this mean we should be praying twenty-four/seven, or is it referring to something else? Read 1 Thessalonians 5:16-19 and discuss what God is telling us.

7 | Some believers who are filled with the Holy Spirit have looked down upon those who have not received this amazing Gift—treating them as second-class Christians. Have you ever been treated like this? If so, how did it affect your relationship with God and other believers? Have you ever treated someone this way, knowingly or unknowingly? What should be our attitude regarding the infilling of the Spirit?

NOTES

CHAPTER SUMMARY:

- Expressions of intimacy with the Spirit, including praying in tongues, have a proper time and place.

- Don't ignore, despise, or abstain from the gift of tongues because some have misused it.

- When you pray in tongues, you are speaking the mysteries of God, and you can ask Him to give you the interpretation of your prayers.

- The Spirit's power is given to the humble. Humility unlocks the door to God's mysteries.

- We can pray in the Spirit when we need wisdom, desire to worship God on a deeper level, or want to intercede for others. The Spirit exponentially expands our abilities in all these areas.

- God's direction often comes in the form of peace; when we pray in the Spirit and have peace about something, the Holy Spirit is bearing witness with our spirits and telling us to move forward.

- Praying in tongues refreshes, rejuvenates, and builds up our entire being. Take time to pray in the language of the Spirit every day!

Bonus Chapter

Q&A

The following content was adapted from a live Q&A session with John and Lisa Bevere. This session is available in audio and video format as part of the Messenger Series on The Holy Spirit: An Introduction.

Lisa: You discussed that some churches have become so focused on developing atmosphere that they neglect the presence of the Holy Spirit. Many churches want to know how they can invite the Holy Spirit's presence again—without bringing back "weird" or unnecessarily long services. How can they do that?

John: Simply ask. As I said before, the Holy Spirit is a gentleman. He leaves it to us to initiate.

Many times, when I am ministering in churches and people come forward to receive salvation, I will say, "Holy Spirit, please touch them." It only takes a few minutes before His presence manifests and people all over the sanctuary begin to weep. I always like that, because the Bible talks about tasting the heavenly gift (see Hebrews 6:1-6), and I find that people are a lot less likely to backslide if they have tasted the heavenly gift—that manifestation of the Spirit's presence.

Once I was in a large church that had transitioned away from some of the forms or manifestations that might remind us of the older charismatic services. In one of the meetings, the Spirit of God manifested His presence. People were weeping all over the sanctuary; God's presence was so tangible. The Lord told me, "Now it's time to tell them to give thanks and praise God." I did so and then closed the service. Afterward, the pastor said, "Wow! I was thinking, *Now we're going to go another hour. We're going to have weird stuff going on, like what used to happen.*" He said, "I love how God led you. When you said that God had finished what He was doing, I could actually feel it, like He had accomplished His purpose. That's when you said, 'Let's close the service.'" I have seen the Spirit of God's manifest presence come in for even two minutes and impact people so deeply.

Lisa: John and I had this conversation recently. Sometimes we only have thirty-five minutes to preach in a service, but the truth is that they are our thirty-five minutes. And so instead of preaching for thirty-five minutes—

John: Preach thirty.

Lisa: Preach thirty. Or give pause for the Holy Spirit in the middle of your message. Give room for the Holy Spirit to actually have His way. Sometimes ministers are busy trying to cover so much area that they forget to let it be saturated by the Spirit.

Lisa: You have shared a lot about what it means when the Holy Spirit "fills us," but what about when He forbids us? What does that look like?

John: The book of Colossians instructs us, "Let the peace of Christ rule in your heart" (see Colossians 3:15). Then Romans chapter eight says,

"For as many as are led by the Spirit of God, these are sons of God" (verse 14). The word *sons* in that verse—which refers to both sons and daughters—is the Greek word *huios*, which means "mature sons."[1] Not every Christian is led by the Spirit. Many are led by their emotions, their intellect, or by situations or circumstances. God was saying that *mature sons and daughters* are led by the Spirit. How does the Spirit lead us? He bears witness in our spirits (verse 16). So in other words, let's say I want to go to a particular city, and I feel a gnawing, itching—almost irritating—scratching in my spirit—

Lisa: Has that ever happened, that you have actually gone somewhere you shouldn't have?

John: Yes.

Lisa: What was the fruit of that?

John: The fruit of it was that I said, "I will not do that again"! It was a disaster. I've learned that if I get that kind of a check, I need to stop.

Now, I have been in a situation where I agreed to go to a meeting and afterward felt like the Lord didn't want me to go, but I had given my word. I said, "God, Your Word says that I'm to be a man who swears to my own hurt and changes not. I have to go to this meeting. I need You to protect me." He didn't rebuke me for that. The trip wasn't great, but I could sense His protection.

But it is better for me to first recognize that check: *Don't do it. You don't want to go there.* It is really amazing—you can recognize it. It is so prevalent. And the longer you walk with Him, the more sensitive you are to it.

Lisa: You talked about Dr. Cho and the amazing things he has done, how he has filled himself up by praying in the Holy Spirit. I also know one of the keys that a lot of people don't understand is that Dr. Cho says "no" to a lot of things so that he can guard that time with the Spirit. The Holy Spirit will tell us "no" to some *possible things* so that He can do an *impossible thing* in our lives.

John: You will notice that in the book of Acts, they were filled with the Holy Spirit in chapter two, but then Peter "filled with the Holy Spirit" spoke to the rulers in Acts 4:8, and the believers were "filled with the Holy Spirit" in Acts 4:31. Being filled with the Spirit is not a one-time event. God says, "Don't be drunk with wine, but be continually filled with the Spirit" (see Ephesians 5:18 AMP). It's not that we leak; it's that we want to be saturated with the Spirit continually. There are times in our marriage when we are saturated in love with each other. Then there are other times that we've been away from each other and we have to be saturated again.

Lisa: You have to be intentional.

John: It's intentional. So stay filled. Being filled with the Spirit is a continuous thing. And when you're filled with the Spirit, it will manifest by psalms, hymns, and spiritual songs (see Ephesians 5:18-20). You'll find yourself just singing. I've been singing a lot more this week—

Lisa: Turn off the TV.

John: Yes, turn off the TV.

Lisa: Limit other things that are going to drain you.

Lisa: Can all believers operate in the spiritual gifts, or just ministers?

John: I believe every believer has the ability to operate in any gift of the Spirit. If somebody is need of a great miracle, that gift of working miracles can come on any believer. God also puts specific gifts on the lives of certain people, and those gifts operate wherever they go.

Lisa and I knew one individual with a gift of healing that allowed him to specifically minister healing to hearts. People with heart problems would travel from all over the nation to his meetings, and they would get healed. This gift of healing on his life helped him accomplish the ministry he was called to.

But I also think of another friend of mine whose son drowned in a bathtub. He was electrocuted, and he was dead for 45 minutes. My friend said, "John, I prayed for thirty minutes, and nothing was happening. The paramedics were disgusted. Then something hit the top of my head. Somebody else looked through my eyes, and I said to my son, 'You'll live and not die.'" And his son was raised from the dead. He believed it was the "gift of faith" that came on him. That gift was needed at that moment.

Lisa: And he was not a minister at the time.

John: He was a police officer.

Lisa: And he wasn't leading a service.

John: He had just come home from the first service he had ever preached in his life.

Lisa: What I want to make clear is—

John: Believers. Any believer.

Lisa: Any believer who is filled with the Holy Spirit, at any moment in their life.

John: And you don't have to wait for a gift of healing. Jesus said, "These signs will follow them that believe: in My name, they will lay hands on the sick" (see Mark 16:17-18). That refers to when you pray the prayer of faith to get somebody healed. God will honor that because He honors His Word.

Lisa: You don't have to wait until the pastor puts you in the pulpit. You don't have to wait until you corner someone in the lobby of the church. You can actually take the power of God, the promises of God, out into your everyday, ordinary world. And if you feel led by the Spirit to speak to somebody, or touch somebody, or pray for somebody, or be generous to somebody—maybe we should just start with being generous—that would be amazing. We can do that.

John: And that's one of the gifts—the gift of giving, generosity.

Lisa: We know the Holy Spirit came to reveal Jesus. So when we talk about the manifestations we have seen in the last couple decades— shaking, laughing, rolling on the floor, and falling—how are those things revealing Jesus?

John: Well, the Bible talks about unusual signs, but usually they are for a short season. There are times when unusual signs and wonders happen, and they get people's attention and point them to Jesus. What

I find very, very distasteful is when people get more into the manifestations than they do into the "Manifester."

Once when I was in Singapore, a healing evangelist came to the church where I was ministering. He had a gift that manifested with people laughing hysterically. In our service, I could sense that the presence of God was about to fall in this large church. All of a sudden, people started laughing, and it was like you had just taken nails to a chalkboard—that's what I felt my spirit.

Lisa: So it was the right thing, but maybe at the wrong time?

John: I said, "Stop! You camped at the manifestation. You didn't follow the Spirit of God. That's not what He was about to do here. He was about to touch people deeply with the fear of the Lord. Now, we're going to hope that the Spirit of God returns and ministers." Then I had them pray again. The Spirit of God came in and people all over the building started weeping.

What happened in those situations where the manifestations were distasteful is that people almost started showing off. A couple is not going to have intimacy in front of everybody. It is as if people wanted to take the intimacy God had given them and show it off, as if they were saying, "Look at this! We're spiritual." I find that the more I know the Holy Spirit, the more I want to protect Him (His gifts, His ability, and His power) in a respectful, honoring way—not in a way that quenches Him. The Bible talks about quenching the Spirit in 1 Thessalonians 5:19-21. Quenching the Spirit happens when you quench His power and His gifts. Don't do that! But do honor Him. Don't display Him as if He is some cheap influence or power.

Lisa: I want to say that we are asking and inviting God to do whatever He wants to do. I find that the Holy Spirit will sometimes do things in a way or at a time that might be inconvenient, but never with force, never to contrive, never annoying. It is never going to draw attention to people; it's going to draw attention to God—and there is usually an atmosphere and a presence for it.

I was recently with a group of people from all different denominations. I heard some of them mocking the manifestations that I believe had been real at one time, and then maybe got carried forward in hopes that God would continue to bless what He blessed before. The function had gotten lost along the way, but the form had stayed, and these people were mocking it. We're not mocking any of these manifestations. We want everything that the Holy Spirit has, but we want it to be in faith. We want it in decent order, and we want it to be accompanied by God's presence.

Lisa: Is it possible for a person to really feel like they have a peace about something and it not be from God?

John: Yes. Absolutely. If you look at Ezekiel chapter fourteen, God talks about the people who come to Him with idols in their hearts. Now, what is an idol? New Testament idolatry is covetousness (see Colossians 3:5), incorrectly desiring something. People with idols in their hearts will even go to a prophetic person and say, "Please pray over me and speak the word of the Lord to me." God said, "I'll answer them according to the multitudes of idols in their heart" (see Ezekiel 14:4). When I go into God's presence and ask for something, I have to make sure my heart is neutral. There have been times when I have not done this. Because my heart wasn't neutral, I had peace that wasn't from God, and it caused me a lot of sorrow.

That's why I was so glad that Lisa and I were in two different cities early in our time of dating. We took thirty days to pray about whether we should move forward in the relationship, and I was so attracted to her that it took me probably twenty-five days to not allow that attraction to dominate me. But I got to a point in those thirty days that I knew if God said, "No," I would be okay with it. I knew it would mean He had somebody else for me and somebody else for her. Once I reached that neutral point, I started really listening.

If I'm going into my prayer closet and I feel that I'm not neutral, I have to work on that—with the Word of God and prayer—until I am neutral. I need to be able to hear yes or no, because if I'm leaning one way or another, I'm going to get a false peace.

Lisa: We've done this a number of times in seasons of life when we've thought, *It's going to be this, it's going to be then, and it's going to be there*—and then we realize it was none of that. We had to erase the entire board and say, "God, whatever You want."

You talk about a kind of *knowing* that comes from the Spirit. When I was studying for the book *Nurture*, I looked up the word *intuition*. It is formed from the Latin words *in* and *tueor*, which together mean "inward tutor."[2] The Holy Spirit is our inward tutor. He gives us a new heart (see Ezekiel 36:26) and begins to teach us.

Lisa: There are instances in life—with people or situations—when everything looks right and feels wrong. Can you talk about that?

John: Every time I've not listened to that inward tutor—when everything was wrong in my spirit and looked right on the surface—it's been a snare and a trap for me.

Lisa: Is that usually when you have an initial response that you reason away?

John: Yes. Usually that initial response is the Spirit of God. And the same issue has arisen when I've ignored your council, Lisa.

Let me say this to the husbands and wives. When Lisa and I were first married, I would pray for around an hour and a half a day. My observation was that Lisa prayed for ten minutes in the shower.

Lisa: I was working full time!

John: There were a lot of times when I would say, "Lisa, I really think we're supposed to do this. I really feel like we're supposed to do that." And she would say, "I don't feel that"—and she would be right half the time! I was so frustrated.

One day I said, "God, I pray for an hour and a half every morning. Lisa prays for ten minutes in the shower. Yet she's right on more than half of these things."

The Lord told me, "Draw a circle." So I drew a circle on a piece of paper. God said, "Put *x*'s all over the circle." I started drawing *x*'s inside the circle. He said, "Now draw a line right down the middle." I drew a line right down the middle.

He said, "Do you notice about half of the *x*'s are on one side and about half of the *x*'s are on the other side? John, when you were single, you were complete in Me and in yourself. But you became one flesh with Lisa, so that circle represents you and Lisa. You're the left half. She's the right half."

Then God said, "Do you know what the *x*'s are? They represent information that you need from Me so you can make wise decisions. The problem is that you're making all your decisions based on half of the information. You need to learn how to draw out of your wife what I show her so that you, as the head of the home, can make decisions with all of the information."

With that insight regarding intuition, I will say, yes, it's come back to bite me when I felt an initial check and ignored it. But there have also been times when Lisa said things that I ignored, even though I knew deep down her words were of the Spirit—because what does He do? He bears witness.

Lisa has also said things—and this happens only once every few years—that I know, *That's not faith-motivated. That's fear speaking. I'm not going with that.* But most of the time when Lisa speaks, deep in my spirit I know, *She's right.* If I ignore that witness, I am the one who pays the price.

Lisa: I think John's being very generous, but I want people to understand that when God speaks something to them, they can trust it. Researchers are saying that the spirit is way more precognitive than we actually understand. When we jump in with our own understanding and begin to second-guess things, we're not doubting ourselves. We are doubting God. When God begins to say something to us, we need to go with it.

I recently had an experience with a group of people on a bus—and I have to say, I hate buses. Our group was on a bus at an airport for a really long time, and one person in the group just couldn't seem to find her way to where all of us had been picked up. We kept calling her, but we couldn't find her.

Finally I saw this person who was jumping up and down and waving their hands, way off in the distance by the taxis, not where we were supposed to be. I wanted to be annoyed with her. But as soon as I looked at her, I thought, *I love her*. It was an immediate heart connection. As soon as I saw her, I loved her, and we made such a strong connection.

God will give you those kinds of connections. Everything in the natural said, *Why would I love her?* But I did. I got a long email from her today. She said, "You loved me right away, and your loving me right away made me feel the love of God in one of the loneliest times of my life." This is what comes from us simply being people who will go by those kinds of connections, instead of letting our environments dictate us.

There have also been times when John has told me, "Lisa, I don't feel good about that person." I responded, "Baby, you just aren't a woman. You just don't know these things like I do." He's warned me like that probably three or four times, and the times I haven't listened, it's come back to bite me.

John: So let me say this: in Acts 15, Paul and Barnabas face some controversy over whether Gentile believers have to follow the Law of Moses. The church sends them to Jerusalem to meet with the apostles and elders. Why don't Barnabas and Paul make the decision themselves? Why do they have to go down to Jerusalem and get together with all the guys? Because power and direction accompany unity. For this reason, husbands and wives should do everything within their power to remain unified. This state of unity makes it possible for us to get clear answers from God.

Lisa: What is the difference between the *gifts* of the Spirit and the *fruit* of the Spirit?

John: A gift of the Spirit is something that God puts upon somebody's life. It doesn't need to be cultivated or developed. It automatically operates. The only thing that needs to be cultivated is *how* the person operates in it. In contrast, the fruit of the Spirit has to be cultivated. So gifts are given, fruit is cultivated.

The fruit of the Spirit is the result of a Spirit-led life. When you walk in the Spirit, the fruit that is cultivated is that you become a person of greater joy, greater peace, greater patience, greater love, etc. (see Galatians 5:22-23). That love, joy, or peace is going to emanate out of you because you're walking with the Spirit. It has to do with your personal life. The fruit of the Spirit is the foundation that will keep you safe in your ministry life. The gifts of the Spirit, on the other hand, pertain to your ministry life—and unfortunately many people pursue the gifts over the fruit.

I have prayed, "God, I never want the gifts You've placed on my life to supersede the fruit You've developed in me." I prayed that so I can finish well, because what often happens is that people start pursuing the gifts. The Bible says, "Pursue love, and desire spiritual gifts" (1 Corinthians 14:1). People pursue the gifts, but they ignore the fruit (love).

Gifts don't have the character to carry people and can end up destroying them. Judas cast out devils. He healed the sick. Yet Judas is in hell. Jesus said, "It would be better for him if he had never been born" (Matthew 26:24 NET). Judas had the gifts of the Spirit operating in his life, but he obviously didn't cultivate the fruit.

Lisa: Some people operate in powerful gifts, yet the fruit of their lives is in such contrast to the power of the gifts. How does that happen?

John: Just take one look at Balaam. Balaam had the gift of prophecy. His prophecies are actually in the Bible! The words he spoke were the words of God. Yet God had the people kill him with the edge of his sword because he was so wicked and disobedient. King Saul was crazy. He was a madman. At one point, he hunted down David, the anointed of God, to kill him. Yet in the midst of this he prophesied one day with the prophets (see 1 Samuel 19).

The fact that spiritual gifts are operating in a person's life does not necessarily indicate the approval of God. Jesus said, "Many are going to say to Me, 'We cast out devils in Your name. We did miracles in Your name. We did great wonders in Your name, we prophesied and preached in Your name.'" Then He'll say, "Depart from Me, I never knew you—you who practiced lawlessness! You didn't develop the fruit in your life" (see Matthew 7:22-23). The Lord spoke to me one day and said, "Did you notice they don't say, 'But we fed the poor in Your name. We visited those in prison in Your name'? The people who do these kinds of things cultivate the fruit." Cultivating the fruit of the Spirit is a safeguard that positions us to finish well.

I first learned this when I was working for a large church, one of the best-known churches in the whole world. This church was visited by some of the most recognized speakers, and also many not so well-known speakers—the whole gamut of Christian ministers. My job was to pick them up from the airport and host them during their stays. I noticed that when certain ministers got into the vehicle, you felt like Jesus sat next to you. They got up and preached, and you felt like Jesus got up and preached.

Other people would come in, and you would think, *What just happened? Why do I feel dirty? Why is their conversation so lewd?* Then they would get up on the platform and people would be saved, healed, and ministered to. These weren't fake salvations or healings; it was the power of the Holy Spirit. I would think, *God, I don't get this! What is going on? How can they act this way with me only to walk up on that platform and see people getting saved and healed?* That's when God showed me that

Judas proclaimed the kingdom, cast out devils, healed the sick, and did miracles—yet Judas is in hell. Balaam prophesied, but God killed him with the sword. Saul prophesied, but he didn't end well. The Lord told me, "The anointing of God—the gifts of God working in someone's life—is not necessarily a sign of the approval of God." You'll know them by their fruit (see Matthew 7:16).

Lisa: Would you say, then, that the gift is something that comes upon someone's life, and the fruit is something developed inside their life— their inward character?

John: Yes, that's an excellent way of saying it.

Lisa: You talked about being led by an inward peace, and you've talked about feeling a check—that gnawing, uncomfortable feeling when the Spirit forbids you. But some would challenge that God even still speaks to us today. They might believe that He only speaks through Scripture. Do you believe God speaks today, and does He only speak in accordance with His Word?

John: First of all, Paul said to the Corinthian church, "You used to follow those dumb idols" (see 1 Corinthians 12:2). Now *dumb* to us means "stupid" idols, right? What *dumb* actually means in this context is "mute." In other words, the gods the Corinthians served could not speak. Paul said, "The difference is, our God speaks." And He speaks clearly.

How does God speak? The New Testament shows various ways that He speaks to us. First and foremost is the *inward witness*, that sense of peace. That is the number one way He speaks.

Lisa: Even more than through His Word?

John: No, His Word always lines up with that. If you get a sense of peace that doesn't line up with God's Word, don't listen to it. You obviously have wrong motives in your heart; you need to get back to neutral first. The Word has the final say.

Lisa: The Word is always the foundation and the structure.

John: Yes, that is right. So the inward witness is number one. Number two is the *still, small voice* the Bible talks about. Jesus said, "My sheep know my voice" (see John 10:27). The Spirit of God speaks what He hears Jesus saying, and that's the still, small voice.

Some people have gotten into bondage because they started following voices without any inward witness. Any time I've heard the voice of God, the witness accompanies it, and both line up with the Word. We're building a foundation here: Word, witness, voice. If you hear the voice but have no witness, don't listen to the voice. I have been in meetings where people have prophesied over me but I experienced no presence of God, no inward witness. I don't heed those words.

The next way the New Testament says God speaks to us is through *dreams*. Acts 16 recounts the story of Paul having a dream. A Macedonian man came to Paul in his dream, saying, "Please come help us." That was the Holy Spirit using a dream to tell Paul, "Get over to Macedonia." God speaks to some people through dreams a little bit more than He does others. God speaks to my wife powerfully through dreams. God usually speaks to me through the inward witness and the still, small voice.

The next way that the Bible talks about God speaking to people is through *visions*. Paul also had a vision. When he described it, he said,

"I don't know whether I was in the body or out of the body" (see 2 Corinthians 12:2). In a vision, you don't know whether you're in the body or out of the body, but you literally see into the spirit world. When my pastor launched Lisa and me into the ministry in 1989, it was because of a vision. He came into a staff meeting and said, "I had a vision last night. It was like I was watching it on a TV screen. One of you pastors will not be on our staff much longer. You'll be traveling all over, and you'll be a blessing to the Body of Christ." Then he said, "That man is you, John Bevere." God had told me the same thing in prayer about eight months earlier, so it was a confirmation to me.

The final way the New Testament says God speaks to us is through *trances*. Peter experienced a trance in Acts 10. A trance is when your senses are suspended. This is different from a vision, because in a vision, your senses are still intact—you can move around. When Paul and John went up to heaven, they moved around. In a trance, you *see* something and you *hear* the voice of God. All your other senses are suspended.

Now somebody might say, "But what about a fleece?" A fleece is an Old Testament method of hearing God. You have to take everything in the Old Testament run it through the cross. The cross will leave it alone, revise it, or delete it. I take fleeces and run them through the cross, and I see that the cross deletes them. The Bible says, "For as many as are led *by the Spirit of God*," not, "as many as are led by fleeces" (see Romans 8:14). People in the Old Testament didn't have the Spirit of God abiding inside them, so God talked to them through things like fleeces. I personally don't encourage fleeces to New Testament believers. I believe they're okay, but make sure you're ultimately being led by the Word and the inward witness. A fleece is in the physical realm, and you don't want to get messed up by operating in that realm. We are called to live in the Spirit and to walk by the Spirit.

Lisa: I want to add to what you said. All those answers were according to the spiritual realm. We also have a very clear mandate that if you see your brother in need, don't shut your heart (see 1 John 3:16-18). Sometimes you don't need a voice from heaven. Sometimes you just need to *see* or *hear* about a need. When we *heard* what was happening with our books—that people were tearing apart the pages and passing them around—we said, "How can we shut up our hearts?" We had never seen it, but when we *heard* it, we said, "We are going to respond."

John: When I *heard* about girls being trafficked, God didn't speak to me, but I said, "Lisa, we've got to help."

Lisa: I *read* it in a magazine. I *saw* it when I was overseas. Sometimes people are looking for a sign or a trance or a vision or a dream when the Bible says, "If you *see*."

John: "If you see your brother in need."

Lisa: And we start with our brother or sister in need. We start with the Christian in need. We start with the ones we can actually see, the ones we can actually touch, the ones whose voices we can actually hear—and we can't shut our hearts. I find that every time we respond to what we see in the natural realm, God entrusts us with more of the spiritual realm, because He says, "I see you've been faithful with this. I can trust you with a little bit more of the faith realm."

Additional Answers from John

Question: How do you blaspheme the Holy Spirit?

John: Jesus' references to the blasphemy of the Holy Spirit can be found in Matthew 12:22-32; Mark 3:22-30 and Luke 12:10. In Matthew's and Mark's accounts, the context is clearly brought out. The religious leaders accused Jesus of casting out demons by the power of Beelzebub, the prince of demons. That was when Jesus said, "Every sin and blasphemy will be forgiven men, but the blasphemy against the Spirit will not be forgiven men" (Matthew 12:31). Therefore, to blaspheme the Holy Spirit is to blatantly speak evil of Him, in particular to speak of the Holy Spirit's manifestations as if they were the works of the devil.

Question: Is it biblical to pray and sing songs to the Holy Spirit the same way we do to the Father or the Son?

John: Yes, absolutely. The Holy Spirit is God, and He is to be worshiped as God. John 4:24 says, "God is *Spirit*, and those who *worship Him* must worship in spirit and truth." I believe that you should worship and praise the Holy Spirit just like you praise God the Father and God the Son.

Question: How do you know which prayers and/or songs should be addressed to the Spirit?

John: Jesus told His disciples:

> I still have many things to say to you, but you cannot bear them
> now. However, when He, the Spirit of truth, has come, He
> will guide you into all truth; for He will not speak on His own

authority, but whatever He hears He will speak; and He will tell you things to come. He will glorify Me, for He will take of what is Mine and declare it to you....

A little while, and you will not see Me; and again a little while, and you will see Me, because I go to the Father.

...*And in that day you will ask Me nothing. Most assuredly, I say to you, whatever you ask the Father in My name He will give you.* (John 16:12-14, 16, 23)

We petition God the Father *in the name (authority)* of Jesus. Then we fellowship with (meaning communicate and converse with or ask questions of) the Holy Spirit—which is discussed throughout this book.

Question: Is it biblical to ask the Holy Spirit to "come" in a gathering or service when He is omnipresent?

John: Yes. The Bible teaches of both God's omnipresence and His manifest presence. We learn about His omnipresence from David's words:

Where can I go from Your Spirit?
Or where can I flee from Your presence?
If I ascend into heaven, You are there;
If I make my bed in hell, behold, You are there.
If I take the wings of the morning,
And dwell in the uttermost parts of the sea,
Even there Your hand shall lead me,
And Your right hand shall hold me.
(Psalm 139:7-10)

The Bible also says God will never leave or forsake us (see

Hebrews 13:5). Again, this is His omnipresence—His presence that is everywhere always.

On the other hand, there is God's manifest presence. To *manifest* means to bring the unseen into the seen, the unheard into the heard, or the unknown into the known. God manifests His presence when He reveals Himself to our senses (see John 14:19-24). I believe it is biblical to ask for that.

Question: Why do we pray for God to pour out His Spirit? Hasn't He already done that?

John: Zechariah 10:1 says, "Ask the Lord for rain in the time of the latter rain." In Scripture, rain always represents an outpouring of the Holy Spirit. I believe that when we ask God to pour out His Spirit, we're asking for a fresh outpouring on communities, cities, and nations. This is a greater release of His manifest presence, which empowers us to do His work and leads to an increased harvest of souls for God's kingdom.

Question: How can I develop a deeper relationship with the Holy Spirit? How can I experience more of His presence and power?

John: By spending time with God and in His Word. A fuller explanation of how to develop intimacy with God can be found in chapters two and three.

Question: If the Holy Spirit knows all things, why do we need to read the Bible?

John: God gave us His inspired Scriptures because they are "useful for teaching, rebuking, correcting and training in righteousness, so that the servant of God may be thoroughly equipped for every good work" (2 Timothy 3:16-17 NIV). The Holy Spirit uses this written Word (the Greek word is *logos*) to bring His spoken word (*rhema*) to us. The Spirit quickens the *logos* and it becomes *rhema* spoken to us. If we do not spend time in the *logos*—with an open heart to the Spirit—then the *rhema* is much more difficult to come by. The underground church in China was filled with the Holy Spirit, but for years they were desperate for Bibles. They wanted to read God's Word so the Holy Spirit could speak to them through it and bring it alive in their hearts. It is so important that you read the Bible. The Word of God and the Spirit of God work together. It's a partnership.

Remember, the Bible contains the mysteries of God, and the Holy Spirit is the One who reveals those mysteries to us. If you read a passage of Scripture without the influence of the Spirit, you can only see what that text is saying in the language of men. But through the Spirit, you can understand the spiritual meaning of the text, which transcends human understanding, because in the Spirit we have the mind of Christ:

> We declare God's wisdom, a mystery that has been hidden and that God destined for our glory before time began. None of the rulers of this age understood it, for if they had, they would not have crucified the Lord of glory. However, as it is written:
> "What no eye has seen,
>   what no ear has heard,
> and what no human mind has conceived"—
>   the things God has prepared for those who love him—
> these are the things God has revealed to us by his Spirit.
> The Spirit searches all things, even the deep things of God.
> For who knows a person's thoughts except their own spirit
> within them? In the same way no one knows the thoughts of

God except the Spirit of God. What we have received is not the spirit of the world, but the Spirit who is from God, so that we may understand what God has freely given us. This is what we speak, not in words taught us by human wisdom but in words taught by the Spirit, explaining spiritual realities with Spirit-taught words. The person without the Spirit does not accept the things that come from the Spirit of God but considers them foolishness, and cannot understand them because they are discerned only through the Spirit. The person with the Spirit makes judgments about all things, but such a person is not subject to merely human judgments, for,

"Who has known the mind of the Lord
    so as to instruct him?"

But we have the mind of Christ.

(1 Corinthians 2:7-16 NIV)

Question: My church is dry. What can I do as an individual member to bring more of the Spirit into it?

John: Unless you are a leader in your church, the only thing you can do is pray. First, invite the Spirit into your life, so that you bring His manifest presence into the church with you. Second, ask that God would move on the hearts of your leaders to be more open to the manifestation of the Holy Spirit's presence.

DISCUSSION QUESTIONS

If you are using this book as part of the Messenger Series on the Holy Spirit,
please refer to video session 6.

1 | All believers have the ability to operate in spiritual gifts. What might it look like to operate in these gifts outside of formal "ministry" settings?

2 | When you believe God is giving you peace about a decision, what gives you confidence that you are hearing from Him?

3 | Has the Holy Spirit ever spoken through your spouse instead of speaking directly to you? Why do you think He chooses to work in this way, and how can you receive that direction for your life?

4 | When you need to make major decisions and you can't seem to get direction, what can you do?

See Proverbs 11:14; 15:22; 24:6 and Romans 8:26-27.

5 | Do you believe that God still speaks to people today? How has He spoken to you?

NOTES

APPENDIX

How to Receive Salvation

*If you **confess with your mouth that Jesus is Lord** and **believe in your heart that God raised him from the dead, you will be saved.** For it is by believing in your heart that you are made right with God, and it is by confessing with your mouth that you are saved.*

—Romans 10:9-10 NLT

The Holy Spirit longs to commune with you at every moment, encouraging and equipping you to know God and advance His kingdom. But the first step to a life of intimacy with God's Spirit is to receive salvation through His Son, Jesus Christ.

Through the death and resurrection of Jesus, God has made the way for you to enter His kingdom as a beloved son or daughter. The sacrifice of Jesus on the cross made eternal and abundant life freely available to you. Salvation is God's gift to you; you cannot do anything to earn or deserve it.

To receive this precious gift, first acknowledge your sin of living independently of your Creator (for this is the root of all the sins you have committed). This repentance is a vital part of receiving salvation. Peter made this clear on the day that 5,000 were saved in the book of Acts: "Repent therefore and be converted, that your sins may be blotted out" (Acts 3:19). Scripture declares that each of us is born a slave to sin. This slavery is rooted in the sin of Adam, who began the pattern of willful disobedience. Repentance is a choice to walk away from obedience to yourself and Satan, the father of lies, and to turn in obedience to your new Master, Jesus Christ—the One who gave His life for you.

You must give Jesus the lordship of your life. To make Jesus "Lord" means you give Him ownership of your life (spirit, soul, and body)—everything you are and have. His authority over your life becomes absolute. The moment you do this, God delivers you from darkness and transfers you to the light and glory of His kingdom. You simply go from death to life—you become His child!

If you want to receive salvation through Jesus, pray these words:

God in Heaven, I acknowledge that I am a sinner and have fallen short of Your righteous standard. I deserve to be judged for eternity for my sin. Thank You for not leaving me in this state, for I believe You sent Jesus Christ, Your only begotten Son, who was born of the virgin Mary, to die for me and carry my judgment on the Cross. I believe He was raised again on the third day and is now seated at Your right hand as my Lord and Savior. So on this day, I repent of my independence from You and give my life entirely to the lordship of Jesus.

Jesus, I confess you as my Lord and Savior. Come into my life through Your Spirit and change me into a child of God. I renounce the things of darkness which I once held on to, and from this day forward I will no longer live for myself; but by Your grace, I will live for You who gave Yourself for me that I may live forever.

Thank You, Lord; my life is now completely in Your hands, and according to Your Word I shall never be ashamed.

Welcome to the family of God! I encourage you to share your exciting news with another believer. It's also important that you join a Bible-believing local church and connect with others who can encourage you in your new faith. Feel free to contact our ministry for help finding a church in your area (visit MessengerInternational.org).

You have just embarked on the most remarkable journey of intimacy with the Most High God. May you grow in friendship with Him every day!

Notes

Chapter 1

1. James Strong, vol. 1, *A Concise Dictionary of the Words in the Greek Testament and The Hebrew Bible*, 44 (Bellingham, WA: Logos Bible Software, 2009) (hereafter cited as Strong's Concise Dictionary).
2. The content in the preceding section was inspired by R.A. Torrey's book *The Person and Work of the Holy Spirit*. R.A. Torrey, *The Person and Work of The Holy Spirit*, p. 4 (New York: Fleming H. Revell Company, 2010), Kindle Edition.
3. W. E. Vine, Merrill F. Unger and William White, Jr., vol. 2, *Vine's Complete Expository Dictionary of Old and New Testament Words*, 29 (Nashville, TN: T. Nelson, 1996) (hereafter cited as Vine's Expository Dictionary).
4. Ibid., 111.
5. Rick Renner, *Sparkling Gems from the Greek* (Tulsa, OK: Teach All Nations, 2003), 737 (hereafter cited as Sparkling Gems).
6. Ibid., 26.

Chapter 1 Devotions

1. A.W. Tozer, *A Treasury of A.W. Tozer* (Harrisburg, PA: Christian Publications, Inc., 1980) pp. 290- 291.
2. Ibid, pp. 295-296.
3. Andrew Murray, "The Holy Spirit In The Family," *Herald of His Coming*, February 2013, p. 8.
4. Lester Sumrall, *Spirit, Soul & Body* (New Kensington, PA: Whitaker House, 1995) p. 113.
5. R.A. Torrey, "The Holy Spirit's Power in the Believer," see note 3, p. 1.

Chapter 2

1. Spiros Zodhiates Th.D., ed., *The Complete Word Study Dictionary: New Testament* (Chattanooga, TN: AMG Publishers, 1992), s.v. "metochos."

Chapter 2 Devotions

1. Henry T. Blackaby & Clause V. King, *Experiencing God* (Nashville, TN: Broadman & Holman Publishers, 1994) pp. 86-87.
2. Ibid., p. 87.
3. Ibid., pp. 87-88.
4. Brother Lawrence, *The Practice of the Presence of God* (New Kensington, PA: Whitaker House, 1982) pp. 61, 65.
5. Ibid., p. 37.
6. Ibid., pp. 41, 46, 47, 49.
7. Kathryn Kuhlman, *The Greatest Power in the World* (North Brunswick, NJ: Bridge-Logos Publishers, 1997) p. 122.
8. *Sparkling Gems*, p. 116.

Chapter 3 Devotions

1. Francis Frangipane, *Holiness, Truth and the Presence of God* (Cedar Rapids, IA: Arrow Publications, 1999) pp. 56-57.
2. Ibid., pp. 58-59.
3. See Romans 1:17; 2 Corinthians 3:18.
4. C.H. Spurgeon, *All of Grace* (New Kensington, PA: Whitaker House, 1981) p.115.
5. Jeanne Guyon, *Experiencing the Depths of Jesus Christ* (Jacksonville, FL: SeedSowers Publishing, 1975) p. 3.
6. Ibid., p. 11.

Chapter 4

1. Rick Renner, *The Dynamic Duo: The Holy Spirit and You*, 105 (Lake Mary, FL: Charisma House, 1994).

2. Joseph Henry Thayer, *A Greek-English Lexicon of the New Testament: Being Grimm's Wilke's Clavis Novi Testamenti*, 509 (New York: Harper & Brothers, 1889).

3. M. G. Easton, *Easton's Bible Dictionary* (New York: Harper & Brothers, 1893).

Chapter 4 Devotions

1. See Exodus 3:2-4; 13:21; 14:24; Psalm 78:14.

2. Charles Spurgeon, *The Power in Praising God* (New Kensington, PA: Whitaker House, 1998) p. 31.

3. Joseph Henry Thayer, D.D., *Thayer's Greek-English Lexicon of the New Testament* (Grand Rapids, MI: Baker Book House, 1977) p. 517, adapted.

4. Smith Wigglesworth, *Ever Increasing Faith* (Springfield, MO: Gospel Publishing House, 1971) pp. 96-97.

5. Reinhard Bonnke, *Living a Life of Fire* (Orlando, FL: E-R Productions LLC, 2009) p. 237.

6. Ibid., pp. 274, 369.

7. Watchman Nee, *Let Us Pray* (New York, NY: Christian Fellowship Publishers, Inc., 1977) p. 71.

8. Kathryn Kuhlman, *The Greatest Power in the World* (North Brunswick, NJ: Bridge-Logos Publishers, 1997) p. 79.

Chapter 5

1. Spiros Zodhiates Th.D., ed., *The Complete Word Study Dictionary: New Testament* (Chattanooga, TN: AMG Publishers, 1992), s.v. "mysterion."

2. Johannes P. Louw and Eugene Albert Nida, vol. 1, *Greek–English Lexicon of the New Testament: Based on Semantic Domains*, electronic ed. of the 2nd edition., 383 (New York: United Bible Societies, 1996).
3. *Strong's Concise Dictionary*, 51.

Chapter 5 Devotions

1. Kenneth E. Hagin, *Why Tongues?* (Tulsa, OK: Rhema Bible Church, 1975) pp.14-16.
2. Oswald Chambers, *My Utmost for His Highest* (Uhrichsville, OH: Barbour Publishing, Inc., 1997) p. 155.
3. Ibid.

Chapter 6

1. *Vine's Expository Dictionary*, 585. See note under this entry discussing the difference between *teknon* and *huios*.
2. *Noah Webster's First Edition of an American Dictionary of the English Language* (San Francisco: Foundation for American Christian Education, 1967, 1995), 113.

OUR FOCUS, OUR PASSION, OUR CAUSE

-JESUS-

PREEMINENT IN ALL WE DO.

TEACH: to instruct, edify, train, or demonstrate.

Messenger International always has been and always will be committed to the teaching of life-transforming truth. We are transformed through the power of God's Word, so it is our aim to further equip individuals, churches, and leaders through God-inspired teaching.

REACH: to touch, connect, stretch, or get a message to.

We have a dedicated global focus to make these messages available to pastors and leaders regardless of location or financial position. We support this work through the translation and distribution of our resources in over 60 languages and through our broadcast *The Messenger* which reaches into over 200 nations.

RESCUE: to save, free, release, liberate, and restore.

The Church is His hands and feet to a lost and hurting world. Poverty and the tyranny of human trafficking have imprisoned multiplied millions. Messenger International is committed to rescue, restoration, and empowerment both near and far.

MESSENGERINTERNATIONAL.ORG

MESSENGER INTERNATIONAL HAS MADE IT ONE OF OUR PRIMARY GOALS to make our resources available to pastors and leaders regardless of location, language, or financial position. The Cloud Library was created for this purpose.

CLOUD LIBRARY

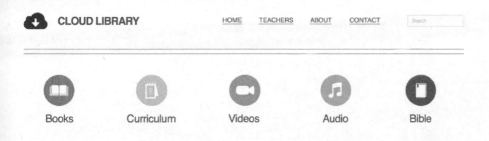

CLOUD LIBRARY   HOME   TEACHERS   ABOUT   CONTACT   Search

Books   Curriculum   Videos   Audio   Bible

WE'VE BUILT CLOUD LIBRARY TO BE an online library where leaders in developing nations can download and stream resources at no cost. It's lean and fast, distributing content to the end-user on edge server locations around the world. The site is fully translated into each language in which resources are available, providing the end-user with an experience that is fully tailored to their native language.

Reduces the risk of those involved with the distribution process

Pastors & leaders can safely & securely download entire curriculum

Travels without restriction

The Cloud Library effect will grow exponentially

Viral: quickly and widely spread or popularized

Unlimited access to life-transforming resources

Reaching the formerly unreachable

To explore and share Cloud Library, visit CloudLibrary.org

THE HOLY SPIRIT
AN INTRODUCTION

To get the most out of this message, gather a group or start a personal study with the six-part Messenger Series curriculum.

Learn about the Holy Spirit's personality and power—and how you can get to know Him better. With five teaching sessions and a special Q&A with John and Lisa Bevere, this curriculum will bring you closer to the eternal God who is passionately in love with you.

Included inside:

- 6 sessions on 2 DVDs and 3 CDs (30 minutes each)
- *The Holy Spirit: An Introduction* interactive book
- Promotional materials

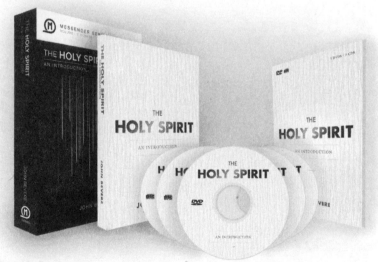

Churches & Pastors

Local churches are the passion and heart of this ministry. Our Church Relations team connects with pastors, churches, and ministry leaders worldwide. It is our joy and honor to encourage leaders, pray for churches, provide life-transforming resources, and build authentic relationships. We'd love to connect with you!

USA: 800.648.1477   AUS: 1.300.650.577   UK: 0800.9808.933

 MSeries.tv

THE POWER YOU NEED TO NEVER GIVE UP

RELENTLESS
CURRICULUM

This 12-session curriculum is designed to instill perseverance and build your faith. Whether you use this study as an individual or in a group, it will help you uncover life-changing truths about tribulation, resistance, and the fulfillment of God's destiny for your life.

INCLUDES:
* 12 30-MINUTE VIDEO SESSIONS ON 4 DVDs
* 12 30-MINUTE AUDIO SESSIONS ON 6 CDs
* HARDCOVER BOOK
* STUDY GUIDE & DEVOTIONAL
* RELENTLESS EXPERIENCE ONLINE RESOURCES
* PROMOTIONAL MATERIALS

THE FEAR OF THE LORD
CURRICULUM

The fear of the Lord is the key to wisdom, knowledge, and intimacy with God. You will be challenged throughout this powerful curriculum to embrace the fear of the Lord in your daily life. If you are ready to grow in your knowledge of God, then this study is for you.

INCLUDES:
* 8 30-MINUTE VIDEO SESSIONS ON 3 DVDs
* 8 30-MINUTE AUDIO SESSIONS ON 4 CDs
* THE FEAR OF THE LORD BOOK
* DEVOTIONAL WORKBOOK
* PROMOTIONAL MATERIAL TO HELP GATHER GROUPS

Extraordinary
CURRICULUM

The *Extraordinary* Curriculum is an extensive journey with 12 video and audio sessions, a thought-provoking devotional workbook, and a hardcover book. As each session builds, you will be positioned to step into the unknown and embrace your divine empowerment.

INCLUDES:
* 12 30-MINUTE VIDEO SESSIONS ON 4 DVDs
* 12 30-MINUTE AUDIO SESSIONS ON 6 CDs
* HARDCOVER BOOK
* DEVOTIONAL WORKBOOK
* PROMOTIONAL MATERIALS

BREAKING INTIMIDATION
CURRICULUM

Everyone has been intimidated at some point in life. Do you really know why it happened or how to keep it from happening again? John Bevere exposes the root of intimidation, challenges you to break its fearful grip, and teaches you to release God's gifts and establish His dominion in your life.

INCLUDES:
* 8 30-MINUTE VIDEO SESSIONS ON 3 DVDs
* 8 30-MINUTE AUDIO SESSIONS ON 4 CDs
* BREAKING INTIMIDATION BOOK
* DEVOTIONAL WORKBOOK
* PROMOTIONAL MATERIALS

HONOR'S REWARD
CURRICULUM

This curriculum will unveil the power and truth of an often overlooked principle: Honor. If you understand the vital role of this virtue, you will attract blessing both now and for eternity. This insightful message teaches you how to extend honor to your Creator, family members, authorities, and those who surround your world.

INCLUDES:
* 12 30-MINUTE VIDEO SESSIONS ON 4 DVDs
* 12 30-MINUTE AUDIO SESSIONS ON 6 CDs
* HONOR'S REWARD HARDCOVER BOOK
* DEVOTIONAL WORKBOOK
* PROMOTIONAL MATERIALS

RESCUED

2 hours on 2 CDs AUDIO THEATER

From the novel *Rescued*

A trapped father. A desperate son. A clock ticking down toward certain death and a fate even more horrible still...

For Alan Rockaway, his teenaged son Jeff, and his new bride Jenny, it's been little more than a leisurely end to a weeklong cruise...a horrifying crash and even more, a plunge toward the unknown...Everything Alan has assumed about himself is flipped upside down. In the ultimate rescue operation, life or death is just the beginning!

AFFABEL
WINDOW OF ETERNITY

2.5 hours on 4 CDs

FEATURING JOHN RHYS-DAVIES AND A CAST OF HOLLYWOOD ACTORS

AN EPIC AUDIO THEATER PORTRAYING THE REALITY OF THE JUDGMENT SEAT OF CHRIST. GET READY TO BE CHANGED FOREVER... AND PREPARE FOR ETERNITY!

This audio dramatization, taken from John Bevere's book, *Driven by Eternity*, will capture your heart and soul as you experience life on "the other side" where eternity is brought into the present and all must stand before the Great King and Judge. Be prepared for a roller coaster ride of joy, sorrow, astonishment, and revelation as lifelong rewards are bestowed on some while others are bound hand and foot and cast into outer darkness by the Royal Guard!

BOOKS BY JOHN

The Bait of Satan
Breaking Intimidation
Drawing Near
Driven by Eternity
Enemy Access Denied
Extraordinary
The Fear of the Lord
A Heart Ablaze
The Holy Spirit: An Introduction

Honor's Reward
How to Respond When You Feel Mistreated
Relentless
Rescued
Thus Saith the Lord
Under Cover
Victory in the Wilderness
The Voice of One Crying

teach reach rescue

Messenger International.

Messenger International exists to help individuals, families, churches, and nations realize and experience the transforming power of God's Word. This realization will result in lives empowered, communities transformed, and a dynamic response to the injustices plaguing our world.

UNITED STATES
P.O. Box 888
Palmer Lake, CO
80133-0888
800-648-1477 (US & Canada)
Tel: 719-487-3000
mail@MessengerInternational.org

AUSTRALIA
Rouse Hill Town Centre
P.O. Box 6444
Rouse Hill NSW 2155
In AUS: 1-300-650-577
Tel: +61 2 9679 4900
australia@MessengerInternational.org

EUROPE
P.O. Box 1066
Hemel, Hempstead HP2 7GQ
United Kingdom
In UK: 0800 9808 933
Tel: +44 1442 288 531
europe@MessengerInternational.org

The Messenger television program broadcasts in over 150 countries. Please check your local listings for day and time.

Connect with John Bevere:

@JohnBevere   facebook.com/JohnBevere.page

MessengerInternational.org